EXCELLING
on a
DIGITAL
TRANSFORMATION
JOURNEY

EXCELLING
on a
DIGITAL
TRANSFORMATION
JOURNEY

A Field Guide To Help You
Define Your Success

Therese Costich

Quality Press
Milwaukee, Wisconsin

Excelling on a Digital Transformation Journey:
A Field Guide To Help You Define Your Success
Therese Costich

American Society for Quality, Quality Press, Milwaukee 53203
All rights reserved. Published 2021
© 2021 by Therese Costich

Publisher's Cataloging-in-Publication Data

Names: Costich, Therese, author.
Title: Excelling on a digital transformation journey : a field guide to help you define your success / Therese Costich.
Description: Milwaukee, WI: Quality Press, 2020.
Identifiers: LCCN: 2020948501 | ISBN: 978-1-953079-91-6 (pbk.) | 978-1-953079-93-0 (epub) | 978-1-953079-92-3 (pdf)
Subjects: LCSH Technological innovations—Management. | Strategic planning. | Success in business. | Organizational change. | Information technology. | New business enterprises. | Leadership—Technological innovations. | Technological innovations—Economic aspects. | Business enterprises—Computer networks. | Electronic commerce. | BISAC BUSINESS & ECONOMICS / Development / Business Development | BUSINESS & ECONOMICS / Organizational Development | BUSINESS & ECONOMICS / Workplace Culture
Classification: LCC HD45 .C6845 2020 | DDC 658.05—dc23

ASQ advances individual, organizational, and community excellence worldwide through learning, quality improvement, and knowledge exchange.

Bookstores, wholesalers, schools, libraries, businesses, and organizations: Quality Press books are available at quantity discounts for bulk purchases for business, trade, or educational uses. For more information, please contact Quality Press at 800-248-1946 or books@asq.org.

To place orders or browse the selection of all Quality Press titles, visit our website at: http://www.asq.org/quality-press

♾ Printed on acid-free paper

Printed in the United States of America

25 24 23 22 21   6 5 4 3 2 1

Quality Press
600 N. Plankinton Ave.
Milwaukee, WI 53203-2914
E-mail: authors@asq.org
The Global Voice of Quality®

To my three kids, Egan, Corrine, and Caris,
who keep me laughing every day and support me
with *almost* every adventure I tackle.

Contents

Note from the Author

I started writing this book in December 2019 when the coronavirus, or COVID-19, was not even considered something of importance. Within a few short months, a pandemic was declared and COVID-19 was taking lives around the world. This deadly virus has resulted in both social and economic disruption.

Our world had already been experiencing industrial disruption (a.k.a. Industry 4.0), but adding this social and economic disruption spontaneously changed how we do business, regardless of whether your business is in financial services, manufacturing, healthcare, or retail.

Social disruption is a term used in sociology to describe the alteration, dysfunction, or breakdown of social life, often in a community setting. Social disruption implies a radical transformation, in which the old certainties of modern society are falling away and something quite new is emerging. Social disruption might be caused by natural disasters, massive human displacements, or rapid economic, technological, and demographic change but also by controversial policy-making.

The term *disruption* often connotes negativity, when it really should be considered an opportunity for eruption. The closing of one door is the innovative opening of another. Now is the time for organizations to create and proliferate (or wither and die).

There are several impacts due to disruption of this level. One is innovation. Innovation usually causes industrial disruption, such as the steam engine replacing the horse and wagon or the telephone replacing the telegraph. What we are currently experiencing with social distancing, home quarantines, "pausing," stay-at-home mandates, and so forth is the disruption that is causing the innovation: innovation to adapt to our "new" life and how we do business.

Another impact is change in both technology and culture (both within organizations and sociology). These changes breed new consumer behaviors, which consequently inspire novel approaches to marketing and selling. Consider the difference in motivation between millennials and previous generations. Consumers are changing; in some ways they are more predictable about their purchases and in other ways they are less predictable.

A third impact is the shift from physical to virtual. The increased awareness and usage of mobile, cloud, and networked communities present a disruptive challenge of selling to consumers who only exist virtually. Consumer pricing questions are just a touch screen swipe away, and the need to react more quickly is more important than ever before.

Leveraging analytics for root-cause analysis, ongoing improvements, and overall real-time awareness of business performance is another impact due to disruption. If organizations are going to survive any form of disruption, being able to make decisions at the speed of thought based on overall business performance and market conditions is not only critical but essential.

FIGURE 0.1   COVID-19 wrecking ball cartoon. Marketoonist, used with permission.

With disruption comes opportunities for everyone and all organizations—opportunities that allow organizations to redefine *how* they work as well as adopt a better way to serve their employees and customers. Disruption is an organization's awakening.

Social and economic disruption during the era of Industrial Disruption 4.0 forces our hand to *be* digital, not just *do* digital. The digital disruption of today compels new thinking and behaviors that end one trend while ironically giving rise to new awakenings that previously didn't exist. As Figure 0.1 alludes to, the pandemic has forced organization's timelines regarding digital transformation to change sooner than originally planned.

Acknowledgments

I wish to thank the following people who provided insight to their world of transformation and went above and beyond supporting me via interviews and examples used throughout this field guide: Peter Federko, Dennis Delisle, Dr. Harry Sax, Fernando Silva, Michael Higgins, David Pritchard, and Roger Mattice. I wish to also thank Abbey M. Young for helping me with several of the graphics.

INTRODUCTION

*You can't go back and change the
beginning, but you can start where you are
and change the ending.*

—C. S. Lewis

The pace of change is faster than we have ever experienced before, yet today will be the slowest we will ever see again. This is not a passing storm in which we will soon return to our comfortable normal. This is Disruption 4.0.

Companies that achieve their digital transformation goals are racing ahead of their competition. This is not industry specific; however, industries that are more highly regulated are adapting at a slower pace.

Gartner states that digital transformation is becoming increasingly important for the survival of businesses, with digital revenues expected to grow from 16% to 37% by 2021.[1]

A successful digital transformation extends far beyond technology. Successful journeys consist of a business-wide culture transformation within both the organization and its infrastructure.

This book is written for the digital transformation leader and the leadership team, and any other member who is undergoing a transformation within their organization, regardless of the industry. It is designed to be educational, informative, and a productive use of the reader's time. Within each chapter are guidelines of items to consider when undertaking a digital transformation journey. Each chapter also provides the reader with questions that, if pondered (and answered), will provide guidance and insight on how to define and embark on a successful digital transformation journey. Readers are encouraged to use the space within the book to capture their answers. It is often said that when something has been written, it holds more validity.

If you have already started your journey, keep reading. This book will provide you with lessons learned from other companies that have undertaken the digital transformation journey. Lessons learned include not only stories of success, but also opportunities for improvement.

Note

1. Alice Pearce, "People, Process, and Technology: 3 Steps to Digital Transformation," January 30, 2018, *Cloud Transformation*. https://everycity.co.uk/blog/cloud-transformation/2018/01/people-process-technology-3-steps-path-digital-transformation/, accessed March 18, 2020.

1

WHAT IS DIGITAL TRANSFORMATION AND WHAT IS IT NOT?

It is not about what it is—it's about what it can become!

—Dr. Seuss

With today's technology and fast-paced innovations, the world is drowning in a tsunami of data. What companies do with the data and how they embrace the rapid changes of industry will shape their journey of digital transformation and, ultimately, their chance of survival.

What Digital Transformation Is

So, what is digital transformation? Is it just another buzzword of today's techie world? Is it just another word for Disruption 4.0?

To better understand digital transformation, a review of the previous industrial disruptions will provide a foundation. Figure 1.1 defines Industrial Disruption 1.0–4.0.

Digital transformation is a component of Disruption 4.0. It is the process that surrounds an organization as it creates its digital platforms linking all sources

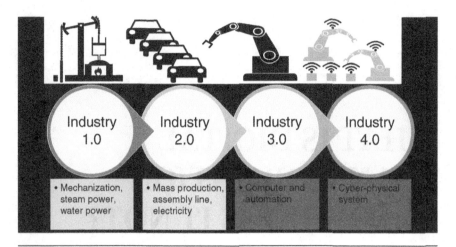

FIGURE 1.1   Industrial Disruption 1.0–4.0.
Source: Vikas Mudgil, "Industry 4.0–The Digital Transformation," *Education and History*, March 17, 2018. https://yourstory.com/mystory/6c9afe6ee2-industry-4-0-the-digi, accessed June 2020.

of data, thereby capitalizing on the sea of information that is engulfing it. It is enabling and empowering its employees to be more efficient and sufficient; to make better-informed decisions using data that are easily accessible; to link visual dashboards across an organization to create a centralized, operational excellence umbrella. It is the changes associated with the application of digital technology in every aspect of our lives as a customer, consumer, or employee.

Digital transformation is about *being* digital versus just *doing* digital. So, what is really the difference? Let's begin by first defining some key terms:

Doing: to perform an act or duty; to execute an activity or amount of work

Being: the way of existing; existence; a living thing

Being is part of an organization's DNA. It is not just something that the C-suite, certain levels within the organization, or functional groups do. It is something that everyone does, from the CEO down through the organization. It is the fabric of the organization woven throughout each discipline. Understanding the concept of being and applying it to your daily tasks is the cornerstone of defining and shaping your organization's digital transformation journey.

Other key terms include *people*, *process*, *technology*, and *infrastructure*. It is important to understand how these words pertain to a digital transformation journey.

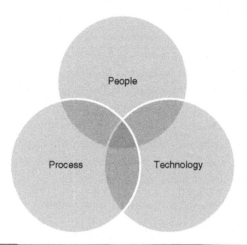

FIGURE 1.2 Venn diagram of the people, process, and technology that create the foundation of an organization's infrastructure.

People, process, and technology are critical components of a digital transformation journey; combined, they create the foundation of the organization's infrastructure. How a company approaches each of these components is crucial to its infrastructure and long-term success. As the Venn diagram shows in Figure 1.2, one component is not stronger or of higher value than the others. Each component can strengthen and add value to the other components by how it impacts the organization.

Listed below are generic definitions for each of these components. Most organizations should be able to relate to the definitions at some level. However, as with any successful initiative, the ideal plan isn't a cookie-cutter approach but rather a well-orchestrated ongoing event with multiple complex parts that are tailored to the organization and its strategic goals.

People

A company culture is composed of its people and is considered one of the most valuable assets of an organization. But to be well orchestrated, the culture has to have the right people with a clear vision of their digital transformation in leadership position. A successful journey requires support from the top down—the C-suite to the custodial staff. "Support" is not just words but also actions and "walking the talk."

In addition to support and sharing the vision of a digital transformation journey, a company's culture also has to have the skill set to develop and implement a digital transformation initiative. This entails understanding all of the integral components and moving parts and how they relate to, and impact, the people, process, technology, and overall company infrastructure. Business, however, is not static; it reacts in a dynamic fashion to market conditions and trends. Organizations need to monitor their progress and performance, and if needed, redirect quickly and with minimal negative impact to the overall health of the business.

A study by Dell computers found that two of the key reasons for digital transformation initiatives failing are people-related. One is a lack of executive support, and the second is a lack of skills within the business to develop and execute the digital strategy.[1] If you have the right people in place, an organization should be able to trust them to make the right decisions for themselves and their work while following the fundamental principles set forth by the company. The other two components, process and technology, are compromised without the right people in place and a shared vision of their digital transformation.

Process

Process is a complex component of the transformation effort. In general, organizations have to change the way they work, go to market, and innovate. They need to stay agile and be prepared for the next turn of events. This, however, is much easier said than done.

Many organizations think that digital transformation or "digitizing their company" is nothing more than throwing technology at their existing processes and automating processes across their business. For a company to be truly successful, this mind-set could be the dagger of death.

A Lean-Six Sigma project at a government contract manufacturing facility focused on reducing part of the financial closing cycle. The team leader of the project started with a SMART (specific, measurable, achievable, relevant, and time-based) goal of automating the process. After two months of working on the project and applying a variety of problem-solving and root cause analysis tools, the project leader disregarded the SMART goal. When asked why, the team leader responded that automating the existing process would be the same old, inefficient process just now automated. The team recognized that the process needed to be streamlined by removing any non-value added steps. Once this was completed, the process went from 20+ steps down to 7 steps, therefore no longer needing to automate a process that was now efficient and "simple."

The spirit of digital transformation is to improve existing processes or create new ones that are efficient and effective for a fast-paced climate. Processes need to be robust and agile to change. Processes, coupled with the people component, need to be designed so that people work more effectively, make smarter decisions based on insight provided by available data, and use the right tools that enable them to be self-sufficient.

Digital transformation impacts every functional discipline and aspect of an organization, including direct interactions with external customers. Therefore, the strategy that is developed for internal processes needs to also take into consideration the customer, how you go to market now, and how you will go to market in the future. This is an opportunity for an organization to envision big-picture outcomes with both internal and external processes, the impact to the customer and what is truly important to the customer, and how the employee can be more efficient in order to have a positive impact on the business and meet the customer's needs more effectively.

Technology

Technology is an enabler of change that can have a positive impact on an organization's transformation. But, despite its capabilities, technology does not stand alone in the digital transformation journey. It supports, and is supported by, the other two critical components: people and process.

Companies have a tendency to buy technology without understanding the overall impact to the organization, its people, and its current processes as well as its future ones. Oftentimes, organizations buy the technology with expectations of retrofitting their people and processes to accommodate the technology. Or, the technology is not tailored for the entire organization, but rather certain disciplines or functions, thereby creating silo data warehouses that are not linked across the organization. This results in the challenge of having multiple versions of the "truth."

Another critical consideration with technology is how it helps the organization achieve its strategic objectives and supports the foundation of operational excellence. Strategic objectives often fall into the categories of financial, customer, operations, and growth. Technology needs to be an integral part of the organization achieving its strategic objectives. The interaction of people, process, and technology can have a direct impact on all four general categories, when considering the speed, efficiency, growth, and response to market trends and the customer's needs and expectations.

If you have been part of any corporate initiative or restructuring, the culture (people) of the company has the biggest impact on the success of the event. Likewise, the culture most likely is impacted the most (and not necessarily in a good way).

What Digital Transformation Is NOT

Before an organization can define what digital transformation means to the organization itself and what it will look like to its enterprise, it is important to also understand what digital transformation is not. Digital transformation is not simply moving files and documents from analog to digital. It is not a code name for layoffs or downsizing or "we are replacing your job with a new shiny robot or computer." Implementation of robotics in industry is becoming more prevalent, but digital transformation with the implementation of robotics is an opportunity for the technical skill level of the employees to also evolve with the new innovation. Employees are considered valuable resources to an organization, not obsolete items.

Digital transformation is not an activity that belongs solely to the IT department. It is not an activity or initiative that only some levels of the organization have to do but others do not. It should also not be considered the "flavor of the month." Digital transformation is definitely not about implementing new technology in the hope that, with this new technology, all of the problems within the organization will go away.

The name, in itself, should be an indication: transformation. Transformation is almost always large and significant. Transformation is an internal fundamental change in your beliefs as to the reasons why you perform certain actions.

Transformation does not require any external influence to maintain because of its fundamental nature. For organizations to be successful with digital transformation, the reward is the same as that for "moving a mountain." If you can move a mountain, you can succeed in doing something that is very difficult and requires a lot of hard work. A good team working together can move mountains.

Defining Digital Transformation for Your Organization

A successful framework for any organization, regardless of the industry, takes into consideration all three components (people, process, and technology) when designing its digital transformation efforts.

Table 1.1 is an example of a template that allows the digital transformation team to better understand what the people, process, technology, and infrastructure look like in current-day operations and what it would look like in digital transformation day-to-day operations. This template is used to start the process and generate discussion so the transformation team members are on the same page. The organization needs to define digital transformation and what it looks like. The information and discussion generated by completing this table will help create this definition.

TABLE 1.1   Example. How does your organization define people, process, technology, and infrastructure *now* and *after* a digital transformation?

General day-to-day operations	Current day-to-day operations	Digital transformation day-to-day operations
People	No clear strategic vision except at C-suite level	Strategic vision and objectives communicated to *all* levels of the organi zation, and quarterly updates and progress reports shared
	Lack of communication about company goals and vision	See above

(continued)

General day-to-day operations	Current day-to-day operations	Digital transformation day-to-day operations
	Lack of analytical skills to convert data into insights or usable information	Training for all levels of the organization on basic analytical skills and interpretation of information and how it pertains to individual departments, functions, and overall operational excellence
	Lack of understanding the importance or use of data and how they relate to "my job"	See above
	"Data and business analytics are not my responsibility" mentality	If employees are trained on the importance of data and the insight the data provide, and empowered to make decisions based on the data, this can change their mentality and make their jobs and day-to-day tasks more efficient for the organization and themselves. It is a win-win.
	Lack of leadership support or visibility	Leadership team needs to instill some basic humble skills and support initiatives throughout the organization. Participate in stand-up meetings, morning market meetings, and lean leader walks.
	Lack of employee buy-in; every initiative is just the "flavor of the month"	Build the trust of the leadership team and empower the employees, assuring them that they have a say in day-to-day operations and the digital transformation journey and vision. Cross collaboration of functions and levels.
	Bureaucracy; employees are not empowered to make decisions or even suggestions	Answer above. Include in employees' performance reviews metrics that tie back to empowerment and ownership.
Process	Difficult to access data; employees are not sure how to use the data for insight	Technology exists that can overlay legacy systems and easily extract the data, allowing for analytics and insight into the process
	Manual processes do not generate usable data	See above
	For processes that do generate data, it is difficult to access the data or IT must be asked to generate a report to access any data	See above

General day-to-day operations	Current day-to-day operations	Digital transformation day-to-day operations
	Validity of the data is questionable, as there is more than one source of data for the same process	Technology exists that can overlay multiple platforms and legacy systems, thereby providing a single source of truth that is easily accessible by all functions across an organization
	Lack of standards and expectations are not known	Ongoing communication and training are critical, especially during a digital transformation rollout
Technology	Database silos	Technology exists that can overlay all legacy databases for a centralized look and feel
	Difficult to access data	See above; technology exists that is user-friendly to access and that will provide insight so the employee or operator can make decisions. Results are empowering people to make the organization more efficient and effective.
	Difficult to determine insight from the data; lack of analytical tools built into the databases	See above; train employees on system, analytics, and interpretation
	Data can be easily manipulated to reflect more positive outcomes	Technology that overlays legacy systems and multiple platforms will prevent any data interception and manipulation. There is a single source of truth.
	The legacy data are old but work for what we need them to do to meet the customer requirements today	Technology exists that will overlay legacy systems and provide a seamless method and still meet customer requirements. Better analytics and interpretation will provide more insight to the customer and better meet their needs.
Infrastructure	Decentralized organization	Centralized organization strives to reach or exceed strategic objectives
	Functional groups within a business unit do not work well together. No cross-functional efforts.	A successful digital transformation requires collaboration across the organization, both vertically and horizontally. It is a team approach that drives success.
	No clear strategic vision except at the C-suite level	Strategic vision and objectives are communicated to *all* levels of the organization, and quarterly updates and progress reports are shared

(continued)

General day-to-day operations	Current day-to-day operations	Digital transformation day-to-day operations
	Different functional groups access different databases, so no one function is using the same set of data, and thus there are multiple versions of the truth	Technology that overlays legacy systems and multiple platforms will prevent any data interception and manipulation and result in a single source of truth
	Partners—is it based on price, product, service, conve- nience? What *really* is the relationship?	Digital transformation requires partners to be cohesive with customer's business outcome needs and willing and able to deliver on those needs in real time (or near real time)

Start defining what digital transformation looks and feels like for your organization. Using the template in Table 1.2, describe what people, process, technology, and infrastructure look like in your organization in regard to general day-to-day operations. Then describe what they look like in regard to a digital transformation journey.

> *When you don't have a vision or a plan for the future, your mind has no choice but to dwell in the past.*
>
> —Steve Maraboli

TABLE 1.2   How does your organization define people, process, technology, and infrastructure *now* and *after* a digital transformation?

General day-to-day operations	Current day-to-day operations	Digital transformation day-to-day operations
People		

General day-to-day operations	Current day-to-day operations	Digital transformation day-to-day operations
Process		
Technology		
Infrastructure		

Note

1. Alice Pearce, "People, Process, and Technology: 3 Steps to Digital Transformation," *Cloud Transformation*, January 30, 2018, https://everycity.co.uk/blog/cloud-transformation/2018/01/people-process-technology-3-steps-path-digital-tranformation/, accessed March 18, 2020.

2

WHERE TO BEGIN?

Well begun is half done.

—Mary Poppins

It is difficult to make a successful digital transformation if you do not even know where you are currently. So, to begin, an organization must first define its problem (or opportunity) statement. This is a simple statement that identifies what the organization will focus on relative to the task at hand. It also identifies the problem or opportunity, current performance, the impact on the company, the impact on the customer, and any relative time frame.

A good statement is specific and quantifies information where possible. Avoid using words or phrases such as *too many, not enough, too long, a lot,* and so forth. These types of phrases are only relative and have different meanings to different people.

When my daughter Corrine was seven, we moved into a new house. A couple of months after our move and after most of the unpacking was completed, my daughter was very upset because she lost her butterfly wallet. When I told her that it was fine and that we would buy a new one, she burst into tears and sobbed that she needed that wallet because she had "a lot" of money in it. Needless to say, she had my attention. Wondering if she had taken money out of my purse, I asked her how much was in her wallet. With her hands on her hips, fighting back the tears, she firmly replied, "I had a lot. . . . I had two dollars!" Now knowing the amount helped define the amount of time I was planning to spend looking for it. Corrine never did find the wallet, and as it had no sentimental value, I did not look for it.

Below is an example of a problem statement for a generic organization that has experienced rapid growth in two years. The statement is not industry specific, but rather is written to provide a general idea of what a statement should look like and what components should be included.

> *Since 2018, our business has grown 65% in both revenue and sales. The number of employees has grown 40%, expanding over 30 countries. Across our operational excellence platform (finance, sales, operations, distribution, quality, customer service, etc.) we are using 10 different databases, or data platforms, to measure and monitor operational performance in the respective areas. None of the platforms are linked, thereby making it almost impossible to understand the true overall operational performance of the company and how it impacts meeting the organization's strategic goals and objectives. Each functional discipline, business unit, or component of our operational excellence framework reports on different information and/or data, making it impossible to understand if there is a single point of truth. Data used for reporting and making critical business decisions are difficult to capture in a timely fashion, often reporting information that is a month old or older. As data are becoming more abundant across our organization, it is critical that every level of the organization be able to easily capture and use all of the data in real time.*

Using the space in Table 2.1, construct a problem or opportunity statement for your organization regarding its digital transformation journey. If you cannot quantify the information now, write it so that the information can easily be included later. This is only the beginning, so do not worry if it is not perfect. Remember, this is a starting point to help establish the direction and focus for your digital transformation journey.

The next step is to determine or define your organization's *current state* relative to the problem or opportunity statement. Current state is best expressed as a detailed list that formulates or supports the statement. Current state is the building blocks of where the organization currently performs or its current operating conditions. It is difficult to move forward or in a different direction if the present conditions are not identified.

TABLE 2.1 Problem statement.

Problem or opportunity statement:

Current State Template

Complete Table 2.2, evaluating *only* the current, existing state of the organization relative to people, process, technology, and infrastructure. Do not conjunct an ideal state or include projected changes or revisions. Be as specific as possible and provide quantified information when possible.

Note: A completed manufacturing example is located in the appendix.

TABLE 2.2 Current state template.

	Current state
People	

(continued)

	Current state
Process	
Technology	
Infrastructure	

Note: this is the actual, current condition, not what you want it to look like or what you wish it looked like. Include as many details and specifics as possible.

> I liken the current situation to that of the Starship Enterprise. The shields are up and the Klingons are shooting at us, and every time they land a punch, they are sapping our power.
>
> —Rupert Lowe

3

WHERE DO YOU WANT TO GO?

Your future hasn't been written yet. No one's has. Your future is whatever you make it. So make it a good one.

—Doc Brown, *Back to the Future*

Many organizations often struggle with multiple systems or data warehouses that "do not talk to one another." When a system or databases are not linked or do not have the capability of being linked, it makes data analytics for the organization difficult and time-consuming, often leading to incomplete information and a less than full understanding of the true business performance.

Dealing with multiple, decentralized systems is probably one of the most common challenges for a digital transformation journey that organizations face, regardless of the industry. Looking back, as organizations began to expand and grow, systems were integrated based on specific functional needs and only in specific disciplines of the organization. There was not an overall long-term data analytics strategy, but rather implementation on an as-needed basis. Since each discipline of an organization has different data and uses of data, the systems implemented were, in general, created for the specific discipline or type of data and usage—thus, ultimately creating a decentralized repository of databases that were never developed to be linked to one another.

As the internet and social media became the world as we know it today, the need for and use of data have become an organization's most powerful tool to provide insight on market trends, consumer behavior and expectations, and day-to-day business performance. Data and data analytics have become critical for an organization's future existence. However, organizations do not want to start over with a single database that links all facets of their business. This would entail replacing existing systems that they depend on for their day-to-day operations. In addition, they have already spent millions of dollars to implement what they currently are using.

So, what would be an ideal scenario for organizations to overcome this common challenge? It should not be up for debate whether an organization will transform, but rather how quickly it will embrace its transformation and implement its new architecture. A successful transformation model will include or highlight data as a valuable business asset that increases the overall value of the company. As an organization starts to imagine (or envision) what it ultimately wants to look like, it should consider how it can turn its data into a revenue stream. One of the important attributes of data is not so much the quantity of data as it is how the data will be used and how they can provide insight to the user and organization.

Determine Your Vision of the Future

For an organization to be successful on the digital transformation journey, it must define where it ultimately wants to go. This is accomplished by having clarity and a vision of its future, embracing the data, leveraging technology and opportunities to stay on the offense, being decisive in this digital disruption, and finally, being resilient to think big and determine what is possible.

Decisions within a corporation should be supported or made using data versus a "best guess." Timely data allow an organization to make a decision that will have a greater impact on the outcome, direction, and focus that will drive success. Having data and all of the information needed at the speed of thought creates an organization that is proactive to rapidly changing market trends.

Scrutinize Key Elements

As an organization begins to formulate what it wants its digital transformation to look like, there are key business questions to consider. These business questions are strategic points that relate to the organization's core areas, values, and strategic goals or objectives. These questions are not cookie cutter in nature, but rather tailored specifically to an organization. The questions encompass the following four components: customer, markets and competition, financial impact, and internal operations and processes.

When considering the customer, understand both internal and external customers. Although the needs of these two customer bases are different, a digital transformation journey needs to have the foresight and robustness to address the needs of both sets of customers. In addition, not all customers are alike. This, too, needs to be taken into consideration, along with how the customer aligns with the organization's strategic direction and goals.

The customer plays a role in both the market and the competition as well. Companies need to be agile and innovative to respond to the ever-changing market conditions and needs of the customer. Over the past several years, the market has transitioned from a retail-driven market to a consumer-driven market. Buying power is now in the hands of the consumer regardless of the industry, including healthcare. In addition, technology has transformed almost everything, including how the consumer shops, works, and plays. Companies need to stay ahead of the technology disruption or they will find themselves falling to the technological prey, similar to many iconic organizations in the past. Organizations such as Kodak and Blockbuster "stuck to their guns" and did not embrace the change that had been eyeing them down for several years.

When reviewing the financial impact of the organization on people, process, technology, and infrastructure, consider the ultimate questions:

- *What is the financial impact if you do not embrace a digital transformation?*
- *What is the financial impact if you "throw" technology at digitizing your business without fully understanding your organization's current state and ideal state?*

- *What is the financial impact of designing an ideal state that takes only today into consideration without contemplating a future disruption?*
- *What is the financial impact if your ideal state is not able to respond to changing market trends and consumer behavior?*

Take a moment to answer these questions. They are simple questions that could potentially cost your organization a lot of money and market share if not answered or considered. The financial impact is woven into every aspect of a business and is just as complex as the consumer.

Internal operations are equally important as the other three components. If an organization is not proactive or responsive to market trends or consumer behavior or competitive threats, that failure can be fatal to its overall survival. Likewise, if internal operations and processes are not updated to correspond to the market, consumer, or competition, this too will be detrimental to the long-term survival of an organization. It is critical for organizations to stay ahead of the market and competition. One way of doing this is to create a robust and agile ideal state.

Always remember, you cannot manage a business you cannot see.

A good template to formulate the questions and help design the desired or ideal state includes these four components and how they relate to the organization's people, process, technology, and infrastructure (defined in Chapter 2).

In Chapter 2, a template was provided to compile a list of current state operating conditions in terms of people, process, technology, infrastructure, and other. This list, if accurate, will provide an organization a clear understanding of its baseline in regard to its digital transformation journey.

Using Table 3.1, imagine your organization's ideal or desired state in terms of people, process, technology, and infrastructure. Take into consideration the pace of change, the multiple sources and abundance of data, and the agility your organization will need to not only survive but maintain a long-term existence following Disruption 4.0 and 5.0, and beyond.

If what you did yesterday seems big, you have not done anything today.

—Lou Holtz

Ideal State Template

Complete the ideal state template, evaluating what an ideal or desired state would look like for the organization. Think *bigger* of what is *possible*. Be specific and provide quantified information when possible. Consider how disruptions impact your business:

- How do you *go* to market?
- How do you *respond* to market trends?
- How *fast* are you able to *evaluate* market trends and patterns?
- How do your employees respond to change and transformation?
- What motivates and drives your employees to be self-sustaining and self-sufficient?
- How is your customer's behavior impacted by disruption as well as the product and service you provide your customer?
- How does your customer's and consumer's behavior change with disruption and innovation?
- How does your organization define "digital"?
- What does "digital" mean to your customer?
- What does "digital" mean to your internal operation?
- How does your organization stay on the offense of industry?
- Are there any constraints to transforming to digital? Are there any constraints or risks for not transforming to digital?
- Does the organization have the right talent for a digital transformation? Does the organization know what the right talent is for a digital transformation?

Note: *Completed manufacturing and healthcare examples are located in the appendix.*

TABLE 3.1   Ideal state template.

	Ideal state
People	
Process	
Technology	
Infrastructure	

4

WHAT IS PREVENTING YOUR SUCCESSFUL DIGITAL TRANSFORMATION?

The question isn't who's going to let me. . . .
It's who's going to stop me!

—Tinker Bell

Any type of disruption can cause an organization challenges. A pandemic, economic disruption, social disruption, Disruption 4.0, and digital transformations are no exceptions. The challenges are usually common to other organizations, regardless of the industry. Common challenges include lack of communication across disciplines as well as from the C-suite down through the organization. This lack of communication includes strategic, tactical, and now, more prevalent, digital visions. With multiple data platforms, it is difficult to identify a single point of truth, making it almost impossible to derive quality and accurate, timely decisions. Reports from across (and within) disciplines often raise questions of whose numbers are right or what data should be used.

Other digital challenges include extracting the data from various databases, especially those with very large volumes of data (*big data*), which add their own complexity and challenges. Often organizations collect volumes of data, but are all of the data useful? Sometimes there are so much data that it is difficult for the user to distinguish what data are needed, what data are useful to derive insight, and what data are meaningless but have been collected since the process was developed and no one has questioned why. Other times, there are useful data that can provide valuable insight, but those that need the information cannot access it because it is too difficult, is too large, or can only be accessed by IT or other disciplines, which adds to the complication of accessing the data in a timely fashion for good decision making.

Another digital challenge is implementing new technology. This challenge has many facets that can bring an organization to its knees. One issue is integrating the new technology with the existing technology without causing logistical issues. Another concern is that the user might not adopt the new technology. There are many ways these challenges can be mitigated with proper planning even before purchasing the new technology.

A critical challenge that all organizations experience is change. For decades, global organizations representing every industry have struggled with change and change management. Change can evoke feelings like uncertainty and fear. Adjusting to change is a very personal thing. Many emotions are involved, and because of that, we tend not to talk about how we are adjusting.

The challenge of change is increased by the lack of proper planning and communicating. Change in an organization can cause stress, resulting in the change itself causing more harm than benefits. There are many different change management models and predictable cycles that people and company culture experience while transitioning. Understanding the predictable cycle and developing strategies for the culture to transition from one phase to another is critical with any transformation.

It is clear that change is a constant, and adapting to change is becoming a fundamental skill required by all employees. Each of us is accountable to recognize how we are dealing with the changes in our lives and to identify what is in our power to move through these transitions.

Change Versus Transformation

When faced with disruption, truly successful organizations do not just change; they *transform*. This means understanding the difference between change or change management and transformation.

> *Change* can be small and incremental, or it can be large and complex; it is *incremental differences made to an existing process over time*, and it is something that *needs to be constantly monitored and maintained*. A conscious external effort is needed to maintain the actions required to achieve the desired result. Change starts from the same mental framework and looks for incremental or modified improvements, not a drastic change or a paradigm shift.

> *Transformation* is a radical rethinking and reconstitution of an existing process, and is usually large and significant. Transformation is an *internal fundamental change in your beliefs* concerning the reasons why you perform certain actions. It does not require maintaining any external influence because of its fundamental nature. Transformation *modifies beliefs* so actions become natural and thereby achieve the desired result, requires a paradigm shift, and results in radical improvements.

How an organization, and its culture, handles the challenges is what defines the outcome and success of its future. But it is not just culture that needs to be taken into consideration for a digital transformation; rather, the process and technology and how all three components interact will truly define a organization's transformation journey.

The next step of understanding how to excel in a digital transformation journey is to identify what is preventing the organization from obtaining the ideal state. This is a time for reflection and soul-searching to understand the interaction between all levels of the culture, the processes that impact the products, services, and customers, and the existing technology. Never lose sight of what the ideal state will look and feel like.

If your organization has not started its digital transformation journey, develop a well-thought-out plan and vision before jumping in with both feet. To create an organizational transformation, it is essential to have dedication and consideration from *all* levels of the organization. This is not a paradigm shift that

FIGURE 4.1 Intern project: developing and implementing a strategic digital transformation plan. Used with permission by Marketoonist.

you can take on as a second-quarter action item with implementation by the end of the third quarter, and not by someone who is part-time or summer help, as Figure 4.1 suggests. The lesson learned that a chief security officer of a large telecommunications company shared was "thinking you can go faster than you can."

Identifying Obstacles to Obtaining the Ideal State Template

Once the identification of the current and ideal states is completed, evaluate what is preventing the organization from achieving the ideal state. Consider the people, process, and technology of the organization. Be cautious not to "throw" technology at the problem or blame a lack of technology or the existing technology as the cause for not operating at the ideal state. As was discussed in Chapter 1, people, process, and technology are components that complement one another and build the foundation of the organization's infrastructure. The three components are stronger as a unit than they are as individual parts.

TABLE 4.1   Template for identifying obstacles to obtaining the ideal state.

	Current state	Ideal state	What is preventing ideal state
People			
Process			
Technology			
Infrastructure			

(continued)

	Current state	Ideal state	What is preventing ideal state
Other			

Please use Table 4.1 to identify what is preventing your organization from achieving their ideal state. Be as specific and thorough as you can, as this is the next critical step for developing a successful transformation strategy and tactical plan.

Note: Completed manufacturing and healthcare examples are located in the appendix.

5

GAPS AND BRIDGES

In the moment of crisis, the wise build
bridges and the foolish build dams.

—Nigerian proverb

Chapter 4 focused on understanding the challenges that prevent an organization from moving from the current state to the ideal state of its digital transformation. The challenges that were identified should be both general and specific, thereby providing a clearer understanding of how the components of people, process, and technology interact with one another and influence the gap between the organization's current state and its ideal state.

In this chapter, basic gap analysis is reviewed as a method of comparing the current state with the ideal state. It identifies gaps between the two states for an organization, thereby aiding in the development of steps needed to close the gaps (or build a bridge).

The first step in narrowing the gap, or building a bridge, is to identify the gap and its associated challenges in the simplest form. The simplest form entails identifying each gap, or challenge, as affiliated with what specific component or components influence the gap. For example, if the organization implements a new technology that will link all of its databases or data platforms so that the communicating and reporting use a single point of truth, but those responsible for selecting the technology chose one that was difficult to learn or made accessing the data difficult or did not take into account a key discipline, then the challenge and gap would include people, process, and technology. People, because it is difficult to learn or access; process, because it did not link *all* of the key disciplines; and technology, because technology was the driver for this example.

Another example would be lack of communication from the C-suite down through the organization regarding the digital transformation strategy and selected future technology. Since this example is only in the preliminary stage of the transformation, the gaps would be influenced by technology (selecting technology before getting feedback from the future users) and people (lack of communication throughout the organization causes uncertainty, lack of trust, and lack of buy-in and ownership).

As an organization progresses through its digital transformation journey, the bridges will become more defined, but initially they can seem very daunting or even impossible. Using the gap template in Table 5.1, complete the gaps and identify the influencers for each of the challenges. Give yourself ample time to identify the influencers, as this will help build a project plan and identify key resources to develop and implement the bridges to close the gaps.

What Is the Gap Between the Current State and the Ideal State?

After the team identifies what is preventing the organization from achieving the ideal state, complete a basic gap analysis. Identify whether the gap and the items preventing achieving the ideal state are associated with people, process, technology, infrastructure, or other. If other, elaborate or describe "other" versus just identifying a generic "other." As was discussed in Chapter 1, people, process, and technology are components that complement one another and build the foundation of the organization's infrastructure. Often, two of the components are impacted by each other and are not singly the only cause of the gap. Likewise, the gap could be a result of all three components, with one component having a more influential impact.

Note: Completed manufacturing and healthcare examples are located in the appendix.

TABLE 5.1 Gap analysis template.

	Current state	Ideal state	What is preventing ideal state	Gap People, pro, tech, infr, other
People				
Process				
Technology				
Infrastructure				

Identify the Bridge to Close the Gap

Innovation: Imagine the future and then fill in the gaps.

—Brian Halligan

After the team identifies what is preventing the organization from achieving the ideal state and completes a basic gap analysis, the next step is to identify the bridge to either close the gap or minimize its impact. Upon completion, Table 5.2 will provide an excellent foundation identifying where the organization is, where the organization wants to be (again, think about big-picture goals), and pathways to achieve its ideal state.

TABLE 5.2   Bridge template.

	Current state	Ideal state	What is preventing ideal state	Gap People, pro, tech, infr, other	Bridges
People					
Process					

	Current state	Ideal state	What is preventing ideal state	Gap People, pro, tech, infr, other	Bridges
Technology					
Infrastructure					

The description of the bridge should *not* be generic but rather detailed; be sure to explain how the bridge will impact the gap. As an organization progresses through its digital transformation journey, the bridges will become more defined.

Note: Completed manufacturing and healthcare examples are located in the appendix.

6

CHALLENGES AND STRATEGIES TO OVERCOME THEM

The moment you give up, is the moment you let someone else win.

—Kobe Bryant

When changes are occurring at lightning speed, the best position for an organization is on the offense. Think big, and always strive to be several steps ahead of the competition. Life, and business, is always full of challenges. Those who can either mitigate the negative impact or simply overcome the challenges have a greater chance of survival. Those who can anticipate the challenges and develop a strategic and tactical plan to avoid them will not only survive, but have a competitive edge in the market.

My mom ran a very efficient home, and she instilled in each of us six kids the necessity to streamline our household processes (a.k.a. chores) but maintain high-quality standards, strive to be the best, and remember the sky was our only limit. One of the common sayings that we heard often in our house was "Don't reinvent the wheel." This chapter is written to help organizations avoid reinventing the wheel.

Below is a list of common challenges that many organizations have encountered either during their digital transformation journey or early on during the planning process. This list was compiled based on information from global organizations representing all functional areas in all industries, including financial services, healthcare, manufacturing, supply chain, education sector, and government.

I am confident that as you read through the list, several items will resonate with you and your organization. To avoid reinventing the wheel, strategies and recommendations for overcoming these challenges from organizations that have experienced them are also provided.

The top five challenges, in no particular order, most frequently encountered across industries, regardless of the size of the organization, are as follows:

1. **Technology**—database silos and decentralized legacy platforms
2. **Culture**—lack of culture buy-in and acceptance, just another "flavor of the month"
3. **Leadership**—lack of leadership buy-in, support, and vision
4. **Organization-wide digital transformation strategy and ownership**—in addition to database silos, business units and functional groups are decentralized from the overall strategy
5. **Conflicting priorities**—not everyone is on the same page, and there is a lot of lip service of support

> *Don't reinvent the wheel, just realign it.*
>
> —Anthony J. D'Angelo

1. Technology: Database Silos and Decentralized Legacy Platforms

I was working in a hospital in upstate New York doing a lean office implementation. During the planning phase, I asked what the hospital was doing with all of its data and how it planned to integrate the data into its lean office initiative and continuous improvement efforts. The conversation quickly turned to all of the "issues" this large hospital (300 beds, over $900 million in revenue) had with its databases. The director of materials management, who purchases more than $50 million annually (spanning 30,000 products and stock-keeping units), started the discussion with the massive quantity of data and limited ability to access any of the information. Another executive in the meeting explained that multiple databases represented the same data set, but had different values depending on what system was being reviewed. Another comment was made on the lack of knowledge or education on how to use the data to make decisions. Needless to say, this hospital, which represented the second-largest affiliate of an overall hospital system, was brought to its knees with the many databases that existed. To make the situation even worse, of the six affiliate hospitals and hundreds of satellite locations, each had the same issues and none of the databases across this healthcare enterprise talked to one another.

A Canadian financial institute also experienced a technology change during its transformation. When developing its tactical strategy, the leadership team did not take into account the overall IT system. They used their old system or platform as-is and *forced* an IT solution around it, in addition to using their old processes that went with the old system. They did not take into consideration how the old processes would work with a new digital solution. They also did not think about how the old processes could be improved prior to any IT implementation. They realized after the fact that if they made the improvement to the processes, the IT solution and implementation most likely would have been different.

Technology: Overcoming Technology Challenges

When developing a technology strategy, it is critical to consider not only the legacy systems and whether leveraging the existing technology is part of the strategy versus implementing a cloud-based solution, but also how the people and processes will be integrated. There are pros and cons to both improving upon the legacy system and implementing a cloud-based solution. Both incur expenses, a culture paradigm shift, security of data, infrastructures, and applications. This field guide will not cover in detail the pros and cons, nor will it recommend one technology over another. A decision regarding which technology solution to use requires extensive research and discussion, and needs to tie into the overall strategic vision for the organization. Regardless of the path your organization pursues, people and processes still need to be taken into consideration when implementing the system.

- Follow these steps for integrating legacy systems or implementing a cloud-based solution:
  - Design a solution or overarching system that spans and encompasses all databases within the organization.
  - Implement a singular platform that is easily accessible for all departments and functions.
  - Incorporate simple analytics and graphical analytics with the platform to provide employees with the tools needed to perform their daily tasks efficiently and with self-service analytics.
  - Train, train, train employees on the analytics and interpretation to empower them to make decisions on process improvement and ongoing continuous improvement.
  - Design the overarching platform to maintain a single source of truth regarding data so that all parts of the organization are working from the same set of data and information.
  - Prevent human intervention of raw data.
  - Protect the data from outside vandalism. Consider restrictions and governance protocols required for government contracts, unions, and the healthcare profession.
- Follow these steps for integrating the people and process:
  - Include the people, who will use the data to provide insight into the organization's performance, when creating and designing the platform that will tie the databases together. The accessibility and input of data needs to be easy, or it will create longer cycle times, inefficiencies, and frustration. One of the underlying goals of a digital transformation is to increase efficiencies, reduce defects and variation, and eliminate waste while maintaining the spirit of continuous improvement and exceeding the expectations of the customers (internal and external).
  - Some processes are more difficult to change due to governances instilled in particular industries. Processes, especially those that require strict guidelines, need to be taken into consideration when implementing a platform over legacy databases (or converting over to a cloud-supported infrastructure). If the processes cannot be conducted while maintaining the requirements and guidelines, then a conflict

of priorities will result (circumventing the new platform to maintain governance).

– Train the employees to use the system. Do not skimp on the training. The quality and efficiency of training will dictate the quality and use of the data to provide insight into business performance. If people are not confident in using the system, it will impact the overall paradigm shift of the digital transformation. According to Cedars-Sinai CIO Darren Dworkin, the healthcare center is undergoing a "large initiative to help support clinical, operational, and research department to enable them to get their data more simply and make it as pre-normalized and pre-translated as possible. Then the experts that understand their area can spend their time analyzing their information."[1]

2. Culture: Lack of Culture Buy-In and Acceptance

It is human nature to be afraid of change. After all, the only people I have ever met who like to be changed are wet babies. So it should not be a surprise when the people you work with, regardless of the level of the organization, push back or ignore the directive, with hopes that this is just a bad dream and tomorrow they will wake up to the same old processes they left the day before. Some employees will embrace the new direction, while others will be reluctant to change their habits regarding how they do their job, how they support their employees, or how they plan a strategy. It is our nature, as humans, to push back when asked to work outside our comfort zone. Digital transformation is a disruption that initially is all about working outside the comfort zone for the greater good of the organization; and with time, new habits will be developed with more efficiency and effectiveness.

Culture: Overcoming Culture Challenges

What do a Canadian financial institution and a crane manufacturer have in common? Their respect, value, and appreciation of their employees.

At Gorbel, a manufacturer of overhead material handling products, fall protection products, and ergonomic conveyor systems, located in upstate New

York, the COO refers to each employee as the "CEO of their area." He respects and values their opinions and contributions to the organization, and is not afraid of sharing his appreciation for them.

The retired CEO of the Canadian financial institution valued his employees so much that he took the time to handwrite a tailored note to each employee during the holidays. He also prided himself on knowing each of their names. Just because he had the title of CEO did not make him better or smarter than the rest of the employees. He recognized that they are the number-one asset of the organization.

Both of these organizations recognized that change is sometimes a requirement to stay ahead of the competition and survive in this fast-paced world. They also understood that not changing could be far riskier for their longevity.

Although it can be difficult to eliminate fear and doubt in people, the leadership and transformation strategy should be designed to mitigate fear and doubt as much as possible. This can been accomplished with a few key tools we all learned in kindergarten during our first week of school. Teamwork, regardless of race, gender, or age, will strengthen the effort to accomplish the goal, as depicted in Figure 6.1.

- Communicate:
  - Convey the digital transformation vision, strategy, and tactical plan to *all* employees.
  - Be consistent and transparent with communications.
  - Communicate frequently via a variety of media (e-mail, town hall meetings, department meetings, morning market meetings, etc.).
  - Keep employees engaged, involved, and informed throughout the entire transformation process.
- Empower and include *all* employees, not just the chosen few or the high-potential employees:
  - Share the vision of the transformation process and final outcome. Allow employees (and the culture) to be part of the vision.
  - Provide the right training and tools to allow employees to be self-sufficient.
  - Incorporate a self-service analytics mentality and tool.

FIGURE 6.1   Teamwork.

— Provide the right incentives and show employees the value of the transformation that will motivate them and hold them accountable. All levels hold some degree of accountability. Failure does not provide an excuse to "throw someone under the bus."

— Train early and continually evaluate training to adjust its effectiveness, if necessary.

— Engage employees to be team members of the transformation, not just spectators on the side. In a Shingo Institute conference I attended, a speaker from Vanguard referenced that every employee in his department is considered a crew member, including him, because they are a team working toward the same goal. Instead of training 1000 "employees," the company trained 1000 problem solvers.

— Employees and operators of the many processes are often the best source of information and operational performance; therefore, include their input.

— Include the employees as part of the decision-making process (this will reinforce a team environment).

— Encourage cross-functional and corporate collaboration—a transformation does not "belong" to only one part of an organization, but the entire organization as a perfectly orchestrated concert.

Practical Application of Overcoming the Culture Challenges

Gorbel, the Canadian financial services organization, Cedars-Sinai Medical Center, Coca-Cola Germany, and many other successful organizations incorporated (or are in the process of incorporating) a model of having data easily visible and accessible to the workforce with a single source of truth. Early success breeds belief and buy-in throughout the organization. Self-service analytics allows for employee empowerment and more timely decision making.

3. Leadership: Lack of Leadership Buy-In, Support, and Vision

The *Merriam-Webster* online dictionary gives the following definitions of leadership and leader:

leadership[2]: the office or position of a leader

leader[3]: a person who leads; a person who has commanding authority or influence

A key driver of the success of anything is a strong leadership team and a leader who is not afraid of failure. For any organization to thrive in the years to come, regardless of the industry or economic disruptions, it must be guided by leaders who are driven to set goals they have no idea how to achieve; successful leaders will determine a way to achieve them in the face of all doubt.

Often, though, some leaders and leadership teams *use* the podium to show support of the various corporate initiatives, but secretly do not "believe" in the initiative. After all, their mentality is driven by running a business and answering to shareholders.

Some organizations appoint a chief technology officer or chief digital transformation officer or chief transformation officer to fulfill the role of transforming the organization to implement a digital ecosystem. Regardless of the title of the role, transformation is a team effort.

Some challenges that several organizations have faced regarding leadership include the following:

- Leadership team does not effectively communicate the vision and objective of the transformation.
- Leadership team "hides" in their ivory towers and do not have an understanding of how the integral parts of the operation work day to day.
- The vision and strategic direction are not always shared by everyone on the leadership team or are considered someone else's responsibility. Therefore, if the transformation fails, it is someone else's fault.
- Not everyone on the leadership team understands the digital vision, and to avoid showing their ignorance, they just do not support the effort or transformation.
- The leadership team at various levels of the organization, including the C-suite, do not perform as a team, sending a strong message of "every man for himself" to the employees.

Leadership: Overcoming Leadership, Buy-In, and Support Challenges

Failure is impossible.

—Susan B. Anthony

As Uncle Ben said to Peter Parker in *Spider-Man*, "With great power comes great responsibility." Leaders are not developed just from their ability to make tough decisions and develop strategic direction, but also from taking risks and going against the grain. They are driven by a higher cause and a complete conviction that they are acting for the greater good.

Below is a list of the tasks and examples that a leader should be displaying for his or her organization in order to have a successful transformation. These characteristics are found already in most executives and leaders. They come naturally to the individual. But, not all people have every characteristic needed to lead the charge during a critical transformation. This list has been compiled based on organizations that have proven success, contributing a portion of their success to the leaders.

- Leaders set the example and share the vision of success.
- The vision of a leader is successful only upon implementation by his or her team.
- Leaders and their support need to be visible at all levels of the organization.
- Leaders need to be part of the solution and ongoing communications.
- Leaders at all levels, including the C-suite, need to communicate the vision and plan via all venues of communication (town hall meetings, quarterly reviews, walking the floor, etc.).
- Members of the leadership team need to hold each other accountable to the vision and goals established by the strategic objectives.
- The leadership team needs to function smoothly as a team, with members supporting each other and sacrificing their own short-term gains for the greater good of the business and digital transformation.

An excellent tool to evaluate a leader's (or any individual) buy-in is a stakeholder analysis. This is a common tool that is used for a variety of projects and initiatives for any discipline in any industry. It consists of weighing and balancing all the contradictory needs of each stakeholder that is involved in the proposed project, task, or change, regardless of the level and quantity of their involvement. It allows for a clearer understanding of any issues or potential concerns and gauges the level of overall support of the initiative.

- Stakeholder analysis:
  - Stakeholder analysis is a process of assessing a system and potential changes to it as they relate to relevant and interested parties or stakeholders (although the use of this tool is not covered in this field guide, an example of a defined template is provided in Figure 6.2).

— Considers the leadership team of the organization and the board of directors.

— Considers any external influences and external leaders (unions, government contracts, etc.).

Organizations that have been successful on their digital transformation journeys had a leadership team that not only was strong but also played a critical and essential role. More organizations around the world are adopting or creating a position of chief technology officer or chief digital officer as they recognize the need for a dedicated position to drive the vision. The vision is owned by the corporation, not just this one officer. If the leadership team performs like a world-class symphony or an NBA Championship team or an Olympic gold medal relay team, the culture of the organization will be quicker to trust the vision and direction, thereby driving a more successful transformation that ultimately results in a paradigm shift.

STAKEHOLDER ANALYSIS

Defining key roles for organizational engagement

Stakeholder	Strategic importance	Current commitment	Involvement	Goals/Needs
Steering committee	Defines and prioritizes use of resources to drive transformation	5	Decision making	• Define ideal customer experience • Define key performance measures • Provide timely information • Guide deployment of efforts
Leadership	Provides resource support and endorsement for transformational leadership	4	Support	• Overview of key activities/service issues • Overview of performance measures • Overview of all activities
Council	Provides a sounding board for decisions; ensures efforts are supported across the organization	4	Guidance	• Participate in surveys • Contribute benchmarking data • Identify existing efforts/initiatives
Operations	Elicit feedback and gather information from all members and their organizations	3	Administration	• Implement strategy • Translate leading practices • Report on successes
Staff	Streamline process and increase capacity; improve brand performance	3	Feedback	• Demonstrate expected behaviors • Support leading practices • Provide feedback on leading practices

Example

FIGURE 6.2   Stakeholder analysis template and definitions.

4. Organization-Wide Digital Transformation Strategy and Ownership

Decentralized Business Units and Functional Teams

Marching band was probably the reason that football was invented, so those who could not roll step and play an instrument at the same time would be able to have some time in the limelight. At least that's what anyone who marched liked to think.[4] The marching band is a component of a football game that keeps striving for perfection regardless of the score, as Figure 6.3 highlights.

I liken an organization, regardless of the industry, to a marching band. There are many moving sections, oftentimes going in different directions, but still striving for a clean and accurate performance. No matter what the role, the effect is lost if the music, drill, and execution are sloppy. A good marching band always aims for precision. Like organizations, marching bands require leadership both for the overall band and for each section. The leader or conductor of the band works with each section leader to establish the vision for each section as well as the vision for the overall band. Without this strategic vision, each section would march aimlessly, wandering around the field doing what they think they need to do but not successfully executing the music or drill. Each musician in a marching band creates sound waves. The waves from each musician, traveling at the speed of sound, reach the other musicians, field conductors, and listeners at slightly different times. If the distance between musicians is large enough, listeners may perceive waves to be "out of phase." Typically, in this case, listeners

FIGURE 6.3 Band cartoon.

perceive that one section of the band is playing their parts slightly after another section, resulting in a *delay* effect.

If an organization does not have a well-defined strategic vision and objective of its digital transformation, each business unit and functional group will "march to its own drum," causing a delayed effect or complete miss altogether.

Some challenges that organizations often encounter with a transformation strategy include the following:

- Different priorities for different business units, or sections, of an organization
- Different priorities for departments with varying functions
- The priorities of some functional departments are not aligned with the organization's overall strategic objectives
- The organization's strategic objectives and digital transformation objectives are not well communicated throughout the entire organization
- The organization lacks strategic objectives or direction
- Projects and programs are not aligned with strategic objectives or direction

Overcoming Lack of Digital Transformation Strategy Challenges

Strategy and goals provide direction for the entire organization. As a consultant for more than 20 years, I am always amazed when I ask someone in the organization what the company's strategic goals are and they repeat the mission statement from five years ago or look at me like the proverbial deer in the headlights.

When I am coaching change management projects or continuous improvement projects, I ask the project manager what strategic goal their project ties back to. Again, I get the "deer in the headlights" look. I always find it surprising that people in an organization will work on a particular project or agree to a set of annual performance metrics but have no idea about the organization's strategic goals and how their daily work ties into helping the enterprise achieve those goals. Strategic goals and objectives should not be a secret reserved only for leadership. Everyone in the organization should know and understand how their day-to-day tasks and operations have a positive impact on achieving these goals. Here are some very basic ways of overcoming a lack of strategic vision and goals for an organization-wide digital transformation:

- The leadership team across the organization develops a set of goals and communicates the goals and vision to *everyone*.

- Strategic goals, especially those pertaining to digital transformation, are linked to everyone's annual performance metrics. Communicate the metrics with each person and confirm understanding and clarification of the importance of their role, to the organization, in achieving the strategic objectives and vision.

- Create the strategic goals and objectives for the organization so all disciplines, functional areas, and business units have a significant role in the digital transformation. Just like a marching band, everyone needs to understand the high step, the glide step, the lateral marching, and when to change direction. The entire organization needs to stay in step toward reaching the goals. The strategy does not belong to one section of the band, or one function department, but the entire organization across all business units.

- As the leadership team develops their strategic goals and digital transformation vision, the organization structure should remain agile. The new frontier of technology, the massive amount of data and information, and the customer experience will require organizations to stay fluid.

- Strategic goals and the digital transformation vision should be communicated effectively and often with ongoing training for everyone in the organization.

Establishing the vision across the organization and ongoing communication will help provide the direction to the entire culture, thereby making the digital transformation a paradigm shift within the enterprise. A chief security officer of a Fortune 200 defense company said one lesson his team learned during their digital transformation was the time it actually took versus the time that was estimated. It was quickly realized that an organization cannot "go buy" the service and immediately use it. In addition, the original estimate completion time did not take into consideration that the skill set and collaboration needed was not available in all areas of the organization (government contracts versus commercial). These critical items needed to be secured and precautions needed to be implemented, which caused additional time for the rollout.

An approach that John Deere decided to try for its digital transformation objectives was to include "forty people from different levels of hierarchy within IT to create the new IT strategy for transforming the company to a digital enterprise," said Ganesh Jayaram, vice president of IT for Deere and Company. John Deere "went through a whole co-creation process before we took it to the C-suite." Some who gave input were new to the company but were subject matter experts in user experience or agile development.[5]

David Pritchard, president and COO of Gorbel, echoed the need for collaboration across all functional areas and having a very clear project plan for rolling out a successful digital transformation. "It is a step by step approach spread across all functional areas in the business. On-going communication of the vision and organizational structure is critical to the overall success," said Pritchard.[6]

"The biggest challenge that Jefferson Health experienced when undergoing their digital transformation was ensuring operational engagement and ownership. The EHR implementation is exceptionally complex and our scope included nearly every workflow, department, and employee. Rather than IT taking the lead in the implementation, we decided to have an operations-led model in which we intentionally gave the clinical and operational leaders ownership of the project. The EHR team provided the project management and oversight of the implementation process while the clinical/operational leaders drove communication, employee engagement, and department accountability," said Dennis Delisle, VP of operations.[7]

5. Conflicting Priorities

It should be simple, right? An organization typically has about four or five strategic imperatives or objectives. Everyone in the organization should have a set of individual objectives for the year such that their day-to-day tasks are aligned with the overall strategic objectives. If they are not aligned, why would someone work on those tasks? Simple question, but one that often receives a convoluted response, as seen in Figure 6.4. Yet, many layers within an organization often work on day-to-day tasks or smaller projects that do not directly, or indirectly, tie back to the strategic imperatives and objectives. So why in the world does this happen?

FIGURE 6.4 Conflicting and ever-changing priorities.

There are many reasons:

- This is how we have always done it, and it works.
- We (I) are too busy right now to stop and learn a different way. Or, we are too busy right now to change direction. Or, why would we change what we have always done. Or . . .
- The director is telling you to work on one thing even though your individual objectives are tied to something else. Hmm . . . the director signs off on your performance review, so what would you do?
- Each department has a different priority, and no one's priorities are aligned with the strategic imperatives.
- Lower in the organization, the strategic imperatives are not communicated, so their priorities are different from those of the leadership team.
- Employees are fighting fires versus focusing on strategic objectives, as depicted in Figure 6.5.

FIGURE 6.5   When you are fighting fires, you cannot always see opportunities for improvement.

Overcoming Conflicting Priorities

It should be simple, right? An organization typically has about four or five strategic imperatives or objectives. Everyone in the organization should have a set of individual objectives for the year such that their day-to-day tasks are aligned with the overall strategic objectives. If they are not aligned, why would someone work on those tasks? (Yes, this is repeated from earlier.)

To overcome this challenge, it is necessary to review overcoming challenges from the digital transformation strategy, vision, and communication. Also, take another look at leadership team support.

If the strategic imperatives and objectives are effectively communicated and directly tied to each individual's annual performance metrics and tasks, then there should be no misalignment. Fighting fires is a sign that a process is out of control. If you find yourself in this situation daily, ask yourself why. The answer will lead you to a better understanding and, hopefully, resolution. Strategic objectives and digital transformation need to be the focus, vision, and main task of everyone's objectives if the company is going to thrive in this world of disruption. If it is the leadership's priority, then it needs to be everyone's priority.

Every organization will have its own challenges that may not be captured on the list provided. The key to success and to stay on the offense is to consider any and all potential challenges the organization and each functional department may encounter. Then, plan and develop a strategy to avoid the challenge or obstacle becoming a reality.

Must-Haves to Overcome Challenges

Obstacles are what a person sees when he takes his mind off of his goal.

—E. Joseph Cossman

Figure 6.6 is a summary of must-haves for a successful digital transformation. It highlights overcoming challenges with the people, process, and technology of an organization, tying back to strategic objectives.

Technology serves as a key enabler to digital transformation. It prompts the question of how to make use of an organization's data to add value to the business and better serve the customers. Digital transformation is not only the adoption of new technology but of understanding the strategies and vision of the

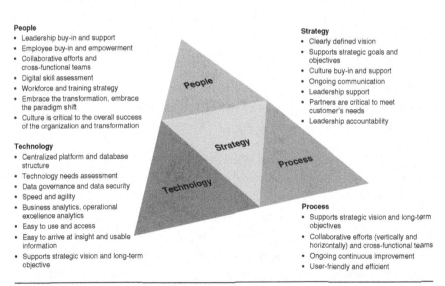

People
- Leadership buy-in and support
- Employee buy-in and empowerment
- Collaborative efforts and cross-functional teams
- Digital skill assessment
- Workforce and training strategy
- Embrace the transformation, embrace the paradigm shift
- Culture is critical to the overall success of the organization and transformation

Technology
- Centralized platform and database structure
- Technology needs assessment
- Data governance and data security
- Speed and agility
- Business analytics, operational excellence analytics
- Easy to use and access
- Easy to arrive at insight and usable information
- Supports strategic vision and long-term objective

Strategy
- Clearly defined vision
- Supports strategic goals and objectives
- Culture buy-in and support
- Ongoing communication
- Leadership support
- Partners are critical to meet customer's needs
- Leadership accountability

Process
- Supports strategic vision and long-term objectives
- Collaborative efforts (vertically and horizontally) and cross-functional teams
- Ongoing continuous improvement
- User-friendly and efficient

FIGURE 6.6   A summary of the items that are needed to overcome common challenges to a digital transformation.

organization, and creating a culture with the right talent and skills to obtain the strategies and fulfill the vision as set forth by the leadership team.

Notes

1. Laura Dyrda, "The Data-Driven Transformation in Healthcare: Cedars-Sinai CIO Darren Dworkin Outlines His Strategy," December 27, 2019. https://www.beckershospitalreview.com/healthcare-information-technology/the-data -driven-transformation-in-healthcare-cedars-sinai-cio-darren-dworkin-outlines -his-strategy.html, accessed July 2020.
2. Definition of leadership, *Merriam-Webster*. https://www.merriam-webster.com /dictionary/leadership, accessed April 2020.
3. Definition of leader, *Merriam-Webster*. https://merriam-webster.com/dictionary /leader, accessed April 2020.
4. Emily Graham, "11 Signs You Were in Marching Band," *Politics and Activism*, April 30, 2016. https://www.theodysseyonline.com/11-signs-marching-band," accessed August 2020.
5. Esther Shein, "7 Secrets for Getting Digital Transformation Right," *Digital Transformation Feature*, November 6, 2017. https://www.cio.com/article/3235958 /secrets-of-getting-digital -tranformation-right, accessed July 2, 2020.
6. David Pritchard, president and COO of Gorbel, virtual interview by author, August 2020.
7. Dennis Delisle, VP of operations at Jefferson Health, virtual interview by author, July 2020.

7

RISK ASSESSMENT

We are now faced with the fact that
tomorrow is today. We are confronted with
the fierce urgency of now.

—Martin Luther King Jr.

Every decision, personal or professional, comes with a level of risk. Depending on the situation, that level can be quantified or arbitrary. Regardless of how it is measured, the risk needs to be taken into consideration when developing a project plan for implementing a digital transformation journey. The easiest and most efficient way to evaluate risk, and develop a tactical plan that mitigates the risk, is to use a risk analysis tool or a strategic planning approach.

There are a variety of different risk analysis tools that identify the risk or failure associated with an action or change, or lack of action or change. Some tools take into account the failure or likelihood of a failure and its impact on other component or process steps within an organization. Some risk analysis tools develop a list of criteria that can be quantified in terms of importance or criticality to the operation. While some tools are subjectively quantitative, others are strictly qualitative. Some apply an elimination criteria, while others focus on mitigating the risk.

The tool that is best for your organization is dependent on a variety of attributes, including culture and complexity. This field guide will describe three tools—failure modes and effects analysis (FMEA), SWOT analysis, and criteria matrix—and provide the corresponding template for the practical application of the specific tool. There are many more tools and methods that are not listed in this field guide.

Failure Modes and Effects Analysis (FMEA)

A very common risk analysis tool is FMEA. There are a few subcategories of this tool, including functional FMEA (FFMEA), design FMEA (DFMEA), and process FMEA (PFMEA). The objective of the risk analysis will determine which FMEA to use. The concept of each one is similar; however, the focus is what differentiates each category of tool.

In general, an FMEA is used to identify and quantify possible process and product failures as outlined in Figure 7.1. It helps to facilitate development and prioritization of actions to eliminate or reduce occurrence of possible failures.

An FMEA provides a structured approach to identify and rank the severity and impact of potential failures. It is a vehicle that evaluates *all* of the possibilities of what could go wrong, why, the frequency with which the failure would occur, the severity to the product or process if the failure occurs, and the likelihood of the failure being detected. All of this takes into consideration the impact on the customer (internal and external). Ultimately, the tool is designed to reduce the risk of failure by identifying and implementing process or product changes early in the program, when it is easiest and the least expensive to correct or revise. Be aware, though, that an FMEA requires hours to complete by a knowledgeable team of the process or product and is considered a "living document." In other words, once improvements are made or the process or product is changed based on the FMEA evaluation, the original FMEA needs to be updated with the latest information. This is ongoing for the duration of the process or product—hence "living."

A process FMEA (PFMEA) is used when creating a new process or changing an existing process significantly. A design (DFMEA) is used when creating a new product or an entirely new process.

Figure 7.2 is an FMEA template that is used globally in any industry. The foundation of the template is an Excel spreadsheet. An FMEA is a combination of

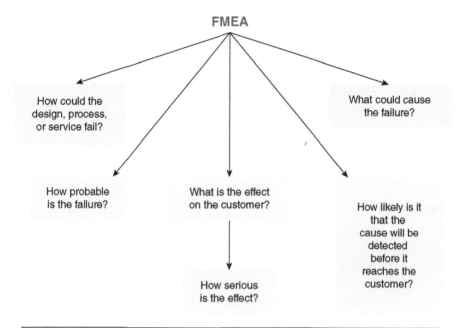

FIGURE 7.1   A schematic of the objective of an FMEA.

The FMEA Form

Process or Product Name:		Airline Reservation Process										Prepared by:		If risk is too high, what can be done?
Responsible:												FMEA Date (Orig)_Feb 27, 20		

Process Step	Key Process Input	Potential Failure Mode	Potential Failure Effects	S E V	Potential Causes	O C C	Current Controls	D E T	R P N	E C
					What are the causes for the failure mode? Ask why.		How can this be found?			
		What can go wrong with the process input/step?	What is the effect on the outputs?							

What is the process step and input?

How serious is such an effect?

How often is the cause likely to occur and result in a failure mode?

How well can we control or detect a cause before it creates a failure mode and effect?

Est. risk is SEV × OCC × DET

FIGURE 7.2   A general FMEA template used for any industry globally.

a qualitative and quantitative tool. The Excel spreadsheet foundation allows for the risk priority number (RPN) to be calculated automatically with the mathematical expression of the product of Severity × Occurrence × Detection.

Figure 7.3 breaks down an FMEA template and defines all of the corresponding columns. It is important that an FMEA be labeled with the design, product, or process being evaluated, the team who completed the living document, and the original and latest revision dates (old versions should not be discarded, as they can add value as a historical reference).

Failure Mode

- A way in which a specific process input or step fails. For example:
  - If not detected and corrected or removed, it may cause a negative effect to occur
  - Can be associated with a defect or a process input variable that goes outside of specification

Note: anything that is deemed unacceptable by a customer is considered a failure mode.

Failure Mode

| Item Name: | | Function(s) Responsible: | |
| | | FMEA Team: | |

Process Step	Key Process Input	Potential Failure Mode	Potential Failure Effects	S E V	Potential Causes	O C C
What is the process step?	What are the key process inputs? (KPIVs)	In what ways can key inputs go wrong? (Process fails to meet requirements)	What is the impact on the key output variables (customer requirements) or internal requirements?	How severe is effect to the customer?	What causes the key input to go wrong? (How could the failure mode occur?)	How frequently is the cause likely to occur?

FIGURE 7.3   An FMEA Excel template with a brief definition of each column.

Effect

- An adverse impact on customer requirements or downstream processes
  - A product or process that does not perform satisfactorily

Cause

- A source of process variation that causes the failure mode to occur
  - How a specific part of the process can result in a failure mode
  - Keep asking *why* the failure mode or input failure occurred

Process Step

- The step within the process that is being reviewed. A process step may have more than one row dedicated to its evaluation when completing an FMEA. Note: a row is dedicated for each potential failure.

Effects Analysis

Prepared by:		Phone No:	
FMEA Date (Orig):		(Rev.):	

Current Process Controls	D E T	R P N	Actions Recommended	Resp. & Target Date	Actions Taken	S E V	O C C	D E T	R P N
What are the existing controls that either prevent the failure mode from occurring or detect it should it occur?	How probable is detection of cause?	Risk Priority # to rank order concerns	What are the actions for reducing the occurrence of the cause or improving detection? Should have actions on high RPN or Severity of 9 or 10.	Who's responsible for the recommended action? What date?	What actions were implemented? Include completion month/year. Then recalculate resulting RPN.				

FIGURE 7.3 (continued)

Key Process Input

- A process input variable that contributes a significant or critical impact on the output of a process

Severity (SEV)

- Relative weighting of an effect; how severe is the effect, if it happens, to the customer (internal and external)
- Usually a scale of 1–10
- 1: customer will not notice the adverse effect, or it is insignificant
- 10: customer endangered due to adverse effect; government noncompliance

Occurrence (OCC)

- What is the frequency with which the cause will occur
- Usually a scale of 1–10
- 1: frequency or likelihood of cause occurring is remote
- 10: assured failure based on warranty return data or significant testing

Detection (DET)

- How likely is the cause to be detected if it does occur
- 1: certain that the failure will be found or prevented before reaching the customer
- 10: absolutely certainty that the current controls will *not* detect the failure

Risk Priority Number (RPN)

- Calculated number; product of severity × occurrence × detection = RPN
- It allows the team to prioritize the items to focus on. The higher the RPN, the greater the urgency to reduce or eliminate the failure from occurring.

Note: this field guide addresses only a generic process FMEA. It does not cover the details of a DFMEA or a PFMEA.

SWOT Analysis

Another tool that is often used for strategic planning, if "thinking outside the box" can be used for risk assessment, is SWOT analysis, as shown in Figure 7.4. SWOT is an acronym for strengths, weaknesses, opportunities, and threats. It is a method or tool designed for use in decision-making processes to evaluate a decision or strategic position or plan. It can be used in any decision-making situation when a desired end state or objective is defined. It can be used for an organizational strategy or even a personal strategy. It allows the user to be specific with objectives and/or decision points, and identify internal and external factors

SWOT ANALYSIS

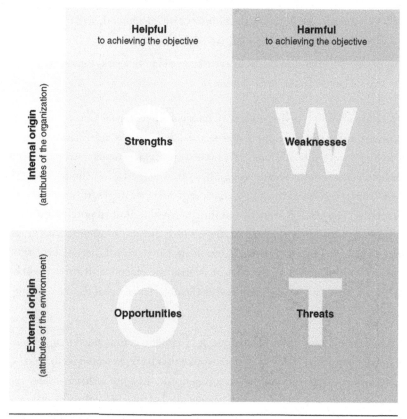

FIGURE 7.4   SWOT analysis matrix template.

that are either favorable or unfavorable to achieving the objectives. SWOT analysis, if completed objectively, promotes discussion and reflection regarding a strategic decision before anything is implemented or the organization takes a particular direction that may be fatal.

Strengths and weaknesses are usually internally related, whereas opportunities and threats are usually focused on external influences. The four parameters are defined as follows:

- *Strengths*: attributes or characteristics that will give the organization a competitive edge or advantage
- *Weaknesses*: attributes or characteristics that will give the organization a disadvantage, are a risk, or will cause a competitive threat to itself
- *Opportunities*: attributes in the industry that, if adopted, will cause the organization to gain a competitive edge or survival
- *Threats*: attributes in the industry that could pose a risk, issues, or a negative influence to the organization

To facilitate a SWOT analysis, identify internal and external factors, select and evaluate or assess the most important factors, and identify any relationships that exist between internal and external features. For example, strong relationships between strengths and opportunities often suggest good conditions in the organization, thereby warranting a more aggressive strategy. Although, strong interactions between weaknesses and threats could indicate a potential warning and suggest using a defensive strategy. Once the four elements, SWOT, are completed and discussed thoroughly, the team can decide if there is a strategic fit and continue on with the project or strategic objective. If there is not a strategic fit, then the team should revisit the objective or goal they are trying to obtain.

When conducting a SWOT analysis, it is highly recommended that a cross-functional team from all levels of the organization be represented so that no stone is unturned. Be cautious not to just generate lists, but rather consider the important and critical factors and attributes needed to achieve the objectives. Also take into consideration priorities of the lists and the interaction of weak opportunities against strong threats.

Criteria Matrix

The criteria matrix is another valuable and simple-to-use tool that is designed to identify the relative importance of process or product characteristics to an overall process, product, operation, and/or strategic decision. It is an effective tool used to provide an analytical and quantitative ranking of prioritization. It allows the user or team to assess and rank a list of options or potential alternatives based on specific criteria. It quantifies the priority of inputs required to achieve outputs,

Description of Required Decision

Criteria Matrix

Solutions or Strategic Decision → Criteria ↓	Weighting (1–3)	Option 1	Option 2	Option 3	Option 4	Option 5	Option 6	Option 7
MUST HAVE								
		☐	☐	☐	☐	☐	☐	☐
		☐	☐	☐	☐	☐	☐	☐
		☐	☐	☐	☐	☐	☐	☐
		☐	☐	☐	☐	☐	☐	☐
		☐	☐	☐	☐	☐	☐	☐
		☐	☐	☐	☐	☐	☐	☐
		☐	☐	☐	☐	☐	☐	☐
NICE TO HAVE								
		0	0	0	0	0	0	0
		0	0	0	0	0	0	0
		0	0	0	0	0	0	0
		0	0	0	0	0	0	0
		0	0	0	0	0	0	0
		0	0	0	0	0	0	0
		0	0	0	0	0	0	0
		0	0	0	0	0	0	0
		0	0	0	0	0	0	0
		0	0	0	0	0	0	0
		0	0	0	0	0	0	0
		0	0	0	0	0	0	0
		0	0	0	0	0	0	0
Total		0	0	0	0	0	0	0

FIGURE 7.5 Criteria matrix template—Excel format.

customer needs, or strategic goals. The method is accomplished by the team identifying and weighing the criteria against each of the alternative options. Establishing criteria forces a group to articulate and examine their values, rationales, and assumptions before making their decision. It is a tool commonly used when evaluating requirements of suppliers, vendors, strategic direction, and so forth (basically any time that more than one option needs to be evaluated, assessed, and rated against others). It provides clarity on attributes or factors that are optional versus required.

It is recommended that the team reach consensus when making a decision if the criteria are identified and agreed on beforehand. This allows for a visual and better understanding of what is really needed versus what would be nice to have versus what is not critical or a showstopper if the option or criteria do not exist. Remember, not all criteria should be considered of equal importance.

How to Complete a Criteria Matrix

Using a criteria matrix template similar to the one in Figure 7.5, there are some simple steps to complete the matrix and prioritize your options to make your decision of direction much easier and with more of a quantified consensus. Note that there are several formats and templates for a criteria matrix. They all differ, but the end result of the tool is the same.

A criteria matrix is completed as a team function using the following steps:

1. Identify the criteria
   - Key factors that matter
   - Determine whether the factors are must-have or nice to have
   - Note: if an option does not meet must-have criteria, it is eliminated
2. Rate the criteria
   - Use a weighting scale approved by the entire team
   - Define each weight (I use 1–3, where 1 has the least weight or importance and 3 has the highest weight or importance; do not use halves—for example, 2 1/2)
3. List the options for the potential solution

4. Rate the options against the criteria and multiply by the weights

   – Rate the options considering how well they fulfill or meet the criteria. For example, if option A fully meets the criteria, it is weighted 3, but if it meets the criteria only partially, it is rated 1 or 2. Multiply the weight of 3 with the rating of 2 for an overall score of 6 ($3 \times 2 = 6$).

   – If an option does not meet the criteria, the rating would be 0. Via multiplication, this would eliminate this option as a viable one.

5. Add the total scores for each option that has been multiplied for each criteria for the overall score

There are many types of risk analysis, decision matrix, and evaluation and assessment tools. Different tools and methods provide similar information but have different ease of use. The tool your organization chooses should be one that best fits your needs. Regardless of the tool or method your organization selects, the effort should be completed by a cross-functional collaborative effort with all levels of the organization represented. A digital transformation is a team effort where the voice of the culture should be represented and heard.

8

LESSONS LEARNED ALONG THE WAY

Every gun makes its own tune.

—Blondie, *The Good, the Bad and the Ugly*

In Chapter 6 we reviewed common challenges that incur during (or before or after) a digital transformation. In addition, we reviewed common advice and recommendations from several organizations on either overcoming these challenges or avoiding them altogether.

While creating this field guide, I interviewed leaders and researched several organizations across different global industries to hear their stories and share their lessons learned. Not all transformation journeys were successful out of the gate. Some took much longer than others but eventually arrived at the ongoing, continuous improvement finish line; others had to hit the restart button a few times before surrendering.

Below are snippets of their stories and some factors that helped drive their ultimate success.

Canadian Financial Services Organization
Company Culture and 100% Leadership Support

The objective or focus of the transformation for this Canadian enterprise was process improvement and making its processes more effective. This was a result of its customer satisfaction survey scoring low for its most valued KPI (key performance indicator). Its journey took about six years, with the organization flailing for the first three years. One of the key things the leadership team learned from the first three years was the importance of the company culture.

The organization incorporated many lean tools, including huddle rooms, morning meetings, and visual management walls. It quickly learned that to be successful with its transformation, more than a tool-based approach was needed. The former CEO believed that an organization needs to "connect to the hearts and minds of the people for the betterment of themselves and customers." He added that demanding change cannot be forced on anyone; rather, one must engage their hearts and minds.

The adage "Changing culture is a marathon, not a sprint" was apparent, as this financial institution quickly learned. But it did not happen without the support and personal and emotional connection of the leadership team from the top down. This retired CEO believed that cultural transformation needs to be led by the CEO; otherwise, they are a barrier.

Initially, not all of the leadership was supportive of the transformation for a variety of reasons. One left the organization on his own accord, while another was asked to leave. Communication and coaching were heightened for the remaining leadership team. The vision, objective, and importance of the leadership team for the success of the transformation was conveyed. It became clear that transformation is very hard work and can be frustrating for all levels of an organization. It is critical for all individuals to believe it is the right thing to do; otherwise, a delay in results will become apparent. Employees did not understand the strategic direction or objective of the transformation. Clearly articulating the purpose and vision is critical, and having a system to communicate it on a regular basis so employees can connect to it is essential and imperative for the long-term success and paradigm shift.

Buy-in and support did not stop with the leadership team. Commitment from the board was also critical for the overall organizational success. The board members were also asked to show their commitment to the employees by rolling up their sleeves and facilitating workshops, leading talks and employee discussion, participating in coaching sessions, and attending morning market meetings and huddle room discussions. This promoted a clear connection to the employees. In addition, the results tied directly back to creating value for the customer. Persistence and patience were required. The organization applied the Shingo principle that ideal behaviors will create ideal results. Respect both customers and employees, and have results tied directly to the principles of the organization by staying true north; it cannot be just about making money.

The now-retired CEO "is stubborn and patient," which are the attributes that allowed him to persevere. He believed in having compassion and mutual trust for his employees. It takes a long time to build trust but only seconds to lose it. By definition, trust is the firm belief in the reliability, truth, ability, or strength of someone or something. Stephen R. Covey, in *The Speed of Trust*, describes trust as the act of building credibility, based on two factors: character and competency. Character is built based on integrity and intention; competency is built based on capabilities and results.[1]

Coca-Cola Germany
Technology and Culture Buy-In

Part of Coca-Cola Germany's digital transformation included consolidating the different locations.[2] At the onset of its journey, it had approximately 10,000 employees with more than 50% customer facing. It had 7 sales regions and 21 plants with more than 80 products that spanned over 500 stock-keeping units. After five years of working (struggling) to implement Systems, Applications & Products in Data Processing (SAP), it realized the world would not wait for it to overcome its challenges with SAP, but rather was moving at a record pace. With social media growing in popularity, the economic power shifted from the retailer directly to the consumer. Coca-Cola Germany realized it had to go direct to the consumer and not retail to grow its market share. It had to "digitize" its business with the objective of increasing market share and sustaining business excellence in a competitive market.

Coca-Cola Germany experienced a paradigm shift in its approach of reporting and tracking operational performance. It centralized its reporting and analytics for the entire organization, regardless of the functional department or level within the organiation. It shifted from a push reporting process to a pull reporting process via self-service and citizen analytics. And finally, it eliminated the capability of manual intervention (or mash-ups) to a single source of truth for the organization's data. As the proverb goes "give a man a fish and you feed him for a day, teach a man to fish and you feed him for a lifetime."

This paradigm shift drove consistent information across all departments from the C-suite down through the organization. It empowered the employees to successfully do their daily tasks while meeting the customer's expectations. Employees executed simple root-cause analysis tools and visualization tools to utilize all data, which were available via mobile, geospatial, and desktop computer.

The truth needs to be in the system. The system needs to be functional and have the power to bring insight and visibility into the business, drilling down to the root cause and solving the problem. Coca-Cola Germany experienced increased process efficiencies in the spirit of continuous improvement. In addition, it experienced the highest market share ever with both volume and revenue.

Jefferson Health, Philadelphia

Culture and Process

Jefferson Health is an academic medical center ranked as one of the best hospitals in the Philadelphia metro area by *U.S. News & World Report*.[3] It is a multistate nonprofit health system whose flagship hospital is Thomas Jefferson University Hospital in Center City, Philadelphia. The health system's hospitals serve as the teaching hospitals of Thomas Jefferson University. "Our health system went through an electronic health record (EHR) overhaul, standardizing information systems (clinical, operational, and financial) to streamline information flow, enhance analytics, and leverage technology to drive efficiencies. The transformation helped connect the health system across sites of service (inpatient, outpatient clinics, etc.) and departments, enabling better communication with staff and patients," said Dennis Delisle, vice president of operations.

Recognizing the effort that it takes to implement a transformation of this magnitude, the EHR team chose to implement the EHR in two waves: the first being the 120+ ambulatory clinics, then subsequently the three hospital facilities. The waves were staggered five months apart.

Jefferson Health's success can be attributed to the employee engagement and ownership at every level of the organization. "We had commitment at the highest levels down to the front-line staff," said Delisle. The executive team recognized that this type of transformation was essential for Jefferson Health's long-term success. "We had a robust change management and communication strategy."

This initiative was different from others that Jefferson Health encountered. It experienced a paradigm shift of its culture and how it approached its daily operations as a result of the digital transformation. "The transparency and ease of information/data flow naturally created a shift in how/what people saw. The new EHR broke down historical and functional silos, provided new insights with advanced analytics, and provided platforms to engage patients in new ways (mobile devices, online access to patient charts, mobile billing, online scheduling, etc.). Since the EHR impacted nearly every workflow, department, and employee it would be impossible to revert back to the 'old way of doing things,'" said Delisle.

As with any digital transformation, Jefferson Health had its challenges. Delisle explains: "The first wave was geographically challenging, as the outpatient offices are spread across three states, though the workflows and systems were not as challenging. The second wave (three hospitals) was a significant lift for the operations/EHR teams and was accompanied with the risk of ongoing patient care (especially for acutely ill patients). Business continuity was a critical focus point to ensure patient safety remained at the forefront. We deliberately took lessons learned from the successes and challenges of the Wave 1 implementation to modify our Wave 2 approach. This led to a well-coordinated implementation and communication strategy, reducing the risk and building end user confidence in the new system."

Other challenges included ensuring operational engagement and ownership. The EHR Transformation Team decided the best approach would be an operations-led model, so they gave ownership of the transformation to the clinical and operational leaders. The EHR Transformation Team provided project management of the implementation while the clinical and operational leaders drove the communication, employee engagement, and department accountability.

Although the transformation team considered every potential challenge and risk, leaving no stone unturned, some things were unforeseen. Some issues were sacred cows or hardwired as "the way we always do it." "It was a challenge to swim against the stream of status quo, though our clinical and operational leaders led the charge in improving processes and workflows so our EHR system reflected best practice rather than current state," said Delisle.

Delisle shared some lessons learned during and after the journey. "The implementation approach is a fundamental step in a transformation journey. It is a means to an end, not the end itself. There is significant work that happens post-implementation to truly leverage the technology, analytics, and other capabilities. The effort expended to achieve a successful go-live is substantial. However it is important to build on the momentum and drive ongoing continuous improvement."

Echoing many other healthcare leaders, Delisle said, "The healthcare industry continues to evolve moving towards a consumer-driven market. Patients demand data transparency, ownership of their medical record, and seamless access. To remain competitive, we (Jefferson Health) needed to adopt the best-in-class EHR and integrate our operations across the care continuum. We had a comprehensive governance model and operations-led implementation approach. This provided leadership and end users a voice in the implementation strategy and ownership in the execution."

Delisle and his colleagues Samantha Inch and Andy McLamb wrote a playbook that was nationally cited as a best practice for healthcare and digital transformation.

Best Buy
Technology, Leadership Vision, and "Digital" Customer Focus

In 2012, Best Buy's stock price was less than $12 per share. Just when Wall Street was beginning to write Best Buy off as a future organization, a new CEO stepped in and developed a leadership team and a strong vision of how to compete in a competitive market where the consumers were holding the power. In order to be a threat in the retail industry, one of the most important factors is to stay relevant and deliver products and services in the right way that the consumer desires. Now, in 2020, just eight years later and during a global pandemic, Best Buy has experienced a historical record-high stock price of over $100 per share.[4]

In 2007, the Amazon business model disrupted retail and how consumers approached purchasing. Showrooms were merely a place for the consumer to look at a product and then go online to shop for better pricing, better delivery, and an overall better buying experience. The consumer was using social media, web channels, and other digital platforms that ultimately controlled the buying power in their favor. Best Buy's business model of showrooms was no longer popular with the digital consumer; it had to pivot to be digitally relevant. Best Buy's digital transformation focused on the customer and what the customer needed and wanted. It created an omnichannel model that essentially made the Best Buy stores warehouses or fulfillment centers, and the front of the store a showroom where new technologies could be viewed and showcased. The customer could touch and feel the newest technology, and because Best Buy had a fulfillment center in the back room, the customer could purchase the product immediately and walk out of the store with the product in hand for insist buyer gratification.

The next part of Best Buy's digital transformation was to leverage the digital platform and utilize the power of technology to improve delivery times and provide an exemplary customer experience. Incorporating a multichannel platform for all types of consumers, Best Buy could satisfy the customer whose preference is to buy online with a 60-minute delivery guarantee for either an in-store pickup or shipped to their location. It was this type of service and focus on the digital customer that differentiated Best Buy from other retailers.

Best Buy's digital transformation model is one of ongoing continuous improvement; by learning from its mistakes as well as learning more about the consumer and the digital world, the better Best Buy becomes at making internal adjustments and improvements to how it conducts business. This led to another key component of the Best Buy model: providing ease of service to the customer. Under one roof, it could provide to the customer a hands-on experience in the showroom, a fulfillment center that could meet the customer's immediate delivery demands regardless of the avenue of purchase, and finally, a technical service center (Geek Squad) that could provide knowledgeable advice and repairs to the consumer. Best Buy focused on supply chain, inventory control, and human connections.

"Digital transformation is not pure digital, but how it is human relatable," said one Best Buy executive. Making technology work for the customer, helping and advising the customer, and then supporting the customer with technical service is the foundation of the digital transformation model for Best Buy, making it the leading retailer in omnichannel business.

Cedars-Sinai Medical Center

Process and Culture

Cedars-Sinai is one of the largest nonprofit academic medical centers in the United States, with 886 licensed beds, 2100 physicians, 2800 nurses, and thousands of other healthcare professionals and staff.[5] This healthcare organization is dedicated to providing high-quality care for any patient. With data registries, Cedars-Sinai formed a team that focused on the quality and governance of the organization's data. They ensured the correct data were getting to the right place and correctly translated to the end user. "One observation we made some time ago was that our CEO became frustrated if he received two different reports on the same issue, which led to two different conclusions. For example, length of stay can have multiple definitions and include both clinical and financial perspectives," commented Darren Dworkin, chief information officer. Dworkin leads the day-to-day strategy and technology operations of the information and clinical technology teams. He led the implementation of a comprehensive electronic medical record system to help transform care using advanced technology, helping to propel Cedars-Sinai to be a national leader in its use of technology at the point of care.

Cedars-Sinai employs a self-service model by providing data to the employees who work with this information every day. "We have a centralized team that manages, builds, and deploys reports for our departments so we can be effective. Then, experts within those areas create dashboards or reports using the data so that team members know the important information and oversee improvements," said Dworkin.

Training on the tools and how to interpret the information and analytics is key. "We teach them how to use the information, and how the information is categorized and defined so they can hit the ground running," said Dworkin.

Gorbel

Technology, Process, Customer Centric

Gorbel is a manufacturer of overhead material handling and fall protection products in the industrial sector, and manufacturer of ergonomic conveyor systems for use in the distribution sector. It is a privately held company that is on the cutting edge of manufacturing—thriving, growing, and always seeking new ways to innovate and elevate its products and processes. Naturally, the next step as it entered the 2020s was to initiate a digital transformation for the entire organization.[6]

"More and more data is becoming available and could be used as a competitive differentiator," said David Pritchard, president and COO of Gorbel. "It was imperative that we had a consistent and deliberate approach for storing, accessing, retaining, and archiving business data. Competitive differentiation, using data and data streams in a predictive analysis models, improving forecasting analysis, and measuring and predicting customer sentiments was the incentive to undergo a digital transformation."

The entire leadership team was on board at the onset. They saw the value and benefits of the data they were capturing (or will capture via a digital transformation). They recognized that having data easily accessible, organized, and supporting innovative technology was critical for the ongoing growth of the organization.

The leadership team knew that in order to be successful, the process of the transformation needed to be correctly planned and implemented with methodical precision. The transformation required a very clear strategic vision that was shared across all functional areas. "Our Digital Transformation initiative was an output from our annual strategic planning process. We communicate to all employees the output from our strategic planning, so it is clear for all in the organization what the priorities are in the business. We also provide updates to employees in quarterly All In Meetings," said Pritchard.

Gorbel did face challenges, including communicating the vernacular about data transformation. "Not all employees are in the know regarding data warehouses and data lakes, or how data transformation can drive a competitive advantage. This communication is important to ensure collaboration in all functional areas," said Pritchard.

The transformation took time and wasn't done with a snap of a finger. The strength that the leadership team brought to the organization was clarity in purpose, understanding the value of such an initiative, and providing resources for support, with monthly check-ins to ensure the project plan was being executed as expected.

McDonald's

Technology, Process, Customer Centric

McDonald's is one of the best-known brands in the world.[7] At one time it was known as the disruptor in its industry, with innovations in standardization, experience in menu and restaurant design, and marketing. As McDonald's was going about its business with day-to-day operations and facing new challenges in product quality, competition such as Starbucks and Subway were investing heavily in digital. McDonald's suddenly found itself behind the digital curve.

To become more of a player in the digital disruption, McDonald's decided that rather than reinvent the wheel, it would hire and assemble an experienced digital transformation team, with employees coming from AOL, Facebook, Yahoo, Microsoft, PayPal, and other various tech companies. This team, and subsequent team members, focused on developing a digital transformation plan that centered on reinventing the customer experience in today's digital age.

In March 2017, McDonald's announced its Velocity Growth Plan. This strategic plan is designed to grow McDonald's wealth and presence in the marketplace with a focus on three key pillars: retain, regain, and convert. Retain existing customers by providing them with what they want and how they want to continue to conduct business with McDonald's (in restaurant dining, digital menus, etc.). Regain lost customers by enhancing convenience and better meeting or exceeding the customer's needs and expectations. And convert casual customers to more committed customers. The integral part of the Velocity Growth Plan is McDonald's digital transformation efforts that encompass three key accelerators: digital, delivery, and experience of the future.

McDonald's digital transformation is striving to deliver a world-class customer experience and profitable growth. Its transformation is not just about adding new technology but incorporating process improvements both inside and outside the restaurant. McDonald's dining areas have been refurbished to include self-service kiosks, table service, delivery, mobile charging points, table-mounted tablets, interactive "magic tables," and more. In addition, the kitchens have been renovated and the process flow has been improved to be more efficient for the employees, thereby increasing the speed of delivery to better meet or exceed the customer's expectations.

Outside the restaurant, McDonald's has redesigned its drive-thrus to be two-lane, making the ordering and pickup more efficient for the employees delivering the meals and the customer ordering and picking up their meals.

These improvements, coupled with their McDelivery, have quickly grown the business from $1 billion to more than $4 billion in three years.

The growth as a result of its digital transformation is unprecedented from any other initiative in recent years. In the first quarter of 2018, McDonald's experienced a 9% increase in revenue and a 13% increase in net income. Just a year later, in the first quarter of 2019, it saw a 5.4% increase in global sales.[8]

McDonald's values its employees and its customers. The improvements to its operations and processes as part of its growth strategy and digital transformation are influenced by the insights of its customers and employees. Other influences that drove the transformation include large technological changes in the industry, customer expectations, and how the power of the consumer and spending habits have shifted. McDonald's continues to see significant growth in both revenue and guest count.

McDonald's digital transformation is an excellent example of what digital transformation is: complementing business processes and delivery with the customer's expectations. The transformation continues to be thorough across the business, employees, and global customer. It has provided the means to the fast-food chain's consistent growth, despite other fast-food chains and casual dining chains struggling. McDonald's has leveraged its digital transformation to drive growth and meet the evolving expectations of the consumer.

Return on Investment (ROI)

What every leadership team has done during the early discussions of digital transformation is to ask the simple, yet complex question, What is the ROI? Once all the capital expenditures are added into the cost and investment equation, while taking into consideration the expected profit, a percentage of the ROI is calculated. The higher the percentage, the more favorable the return. But when evaluating whether to undergo a digital transformation, the deciding factor cannot be just the ROI.

Different organizations have approached this standard question and complicated decision from common points of view. Gorbel decided not to use the ROI as a decision metric for this strategic imperative. The leadership team knew that in order to stay competitive in this growing market, they needed to undergo this critical initiative. Gorbel also recognized the internal efficiencies and ongoing continuous improvement via employee empowerment would benefit the internal operation processes of the organization.

However, Jefferson Health did take the ROI into consideration, according to Delisle. Jefferson Health had a "strategy that included the consolidation and decommissioning of systems, integration of staff, and other efficiencies that the new EHR would enable us to achieve. The investment in systems, equipment, staffing, and support is significant so it was important to clearly outline the ROI. The EHR platform provides the foundation for longer-term success for the health system and was integral to achieving strategic goals that aligned to the evolving healthcare industry and market."

For Coca-Cola Germany, the ROI was never a consideration or "showstopper," according to the former director of business transformation. It was about functionality and the power in which they knew a tailored digital solution could bring insight and visibility into their business.

The ROI of digital transformation is not a "one size fits all" answer. It is more focused on the value generated by changing the way an organization operates, internally and externally, to meet and exceed the expectations of customers, employees, and stakeholders. Organizations approach the investment of "digitizing" against their existing internal operational structure, market conditions, customer, strategic imperatives, and many other factors. The real question in today's highly competitive, digitally driven world is not making a decision based on the outcome of the ROI solely, but rather on the cost incurred to the business if the organization does not pivot digitally.

Notes

1. Matt Harrington, "Trust: A Matter of Competency and Character," Book Review, October 8, 2017. https://www. Benningtonbanner.com/stories/ trust -a-matter-of-competency-and-character,521476#:~:text=By%20definition%20 trust%20is%20the%20firm%20belief%20in,credibility%2C%20based%20 on%20two%20factors%3A%20character%20and%20competency.
2. "Coca-Cola Germany Adds 40–50% to Bottom Line with Help from Salient's Software Solution," Case Study. https://www.salient.com/about/case-studies /coca-cola-germany-case-study-full/, accessed August 2020.
3. Dennis Delisle, interview with author, July 2020. Also see "Transformation and Your New EHR: The Communications and Change Leadership Playbook for Implementing Electronic Health Records," edited by Dennis R. Delisle, Andy McLamb, and Samantha Inch. Boca Raton, FL: Productivity Press, 2019.
4. Ashad Rehman, "How Best Buy and Other Brands Adopted Digital Transformation in Their Business?" *Brandex Marketing*. http://branex.com/blog/how-best-buy-other -brands-adopted-digital-transformation-in-their-business/, accessed July 2020.
5. Laura Dyrda, "The Data-Driven Transformation in Healthcare: Cedars-Sinai CIO Darren Dworkin Outlines His Strategy," *Digital Transformation Feature*, December 27, 2019. https://www.beckershospitalreview.com/healthcare -information-technology/the-data-driven-transformation-in-healthcare-cedars -sinai-cio-darren-dworkin-outlines-his-strategy.html.
6. David Pritchard (president and chief operating officer, Gorbel), interview by author, August 2020.
7. Erin Quilliam, "McDonald's Digital Transformation: Are We Lovin' It?," *Digital Transformation*. https://itenterprise.co.uk/mcdonalds-digital-transformation/, accessed August 8, 2020.
8. Information obtained from https://itenterprise.co.uk/mcdonalds-digital -transformation/.

9

DOING VERSUS BEING DIGITAL

*If you are working on something exciting,
you do not have to be pushed, the vision
pulls you.*

—Steve Jobs

Never will the pace of change be as fast as it is now, and never will it be this slow again! This is not a passing storm, after which we will return to a comfortable normal. Our world has changed—actually, it has been changing in this digital disruption since the 1990s, but with the recent pandemic of COVID-19, the change is unprecedented. So what does that mean for organizations that want and hope to survive the remainder of this decade? It means the luxury of "doing digital" no longer exists. To survive, organizations have to "be digital." *Doing* is a day-to-day task, like performing an act or duty. *Being* is the core of existence. It is the DNA woven throughout the fabric of the organization; and this fabric is worn by everyone, from the leadership team to the cleaning crew.

In a world dominated by digital transformation, the C-suite should understand that operating in the manner of "business as usual" will not bode well in facing the new consumer or customer, or staying aggressive and ahead of their fiercest competitor, which has embraced the digital age. Leaders need to challenge the status quo. Learning from failures (their own or those of other organizations) will minimize the risk and damage their company will incur. Leaders need to be at the forefront of being digital, as it is not just about technology, but how technology interacts and is integrated with people and processes.

When Satya Nadella became the CEO of Microsoft in 2014, he created a culture that focused on "listening, learning, and harnessing individual passions and talents." He also placed employee empowerment at the core of Microsoft's culture.[1]

According to Sandy Shen, senior research director at Gartner, "This (COVID-19) is a wake-up call for organizations that have placed too much focus on daily operational needs at the expense of investing in digital business and long-term resilience. Businesses that can shift technology capacity and investments to digital platforms will mitigate the impact of the outbreak and keep their companies running smoothly now, and over the long term."[2]

In today's world of digital disruption, it is not enough for organizations to merely be up-to-date. They need to be ahead of the curve and embrace the future before it comes. Forward thinking, risk taking, staying on the offense of decision making, and being resilient; these qualities will help organizations that are leaders in global industries be proactive and envision big-picture outcomes.

Notes

1. Marco della Cava, "Microsoft CEO Nadella: 'Culture Is Everything,'" *USA Today*, September 15, 2015. https://www.usatoday.com/story/tech /2015/09/15/microsoft-ceo-nadella-culture-everything/72330296/, accessed May 2020.
2. Laura Starita, "CIO's Should Prepare IT Systems Now to Safely and Reliably Handle a Vast Increase in Remote Workers and Digital Fulfillment of Market Demand," *Gartner*, March 6, 2020. https://www.gartner.com/sma rterwithgartner/coronavirus-cio-areas-of-focus-during-the-covid-19 -outbreak/#:~:text=%E2%80%9CThe%20value%20of%20digital%20 channels%2C%20products%20and%20operations,of%20investing%20in%20 digital%20business%20and%20long-term%20resilience, accessed April 2020.

Appendix

Reading a book is good, but you need to be able to apply what you are reading to make it great and make the changes last.

—Peter Federko

Tables and templates:

- Problem or opportunity statement
- Current state
- Ideal state
- Gaps
- Bridges
- Completed manufacturing examples
- Completed healthcare examples
- Risk Analysis: FMEA, SWOT analysis, criteria matrix

Completed Forms

Current State, Ideal State, What Is Preventing Ideal State, Gap and Bridges Manufacturing Example

	Current State	Ideal State	What Is Preventing Ideal State?	Gap People, Pro, Tech, Infr, Other	Bridges
People	Culture does not support new initiatives because of historical "flavor of the month"	People embrace the transformation and recognize this is the future for the organization (a paradigm shift)	Historical interaction and visual appearances of leadership teams, failed initiatives, or initiatives that faded as the push to increase sales arose	People Infrastructure	Communication of vision, strong leadership, collaboration (vertically and horizontally) for creating digital transformation strategy and roll-out
	People do not support new initiatives because "it won't work here, we have tried that before" mentality	People embrace the transformation and recognize this is the future for the organization (a paradigm shift)	Historical mentality, attitude, and lack of prior support	People	Communication of vision, strong leadership, collaboration (vertically and horizontally) for creating digital transformation strategy and roll-out
	Employees do not feel valued by leadership, do not trust the leadership	Leadership shows more outward value to employees via recognition, morning market meetings, stand-up meetings, project reviews, etc., thereby gaining trust	Historical attitudes and visual appearances by leadership team	People Infrastructure	Collaboration (vertically and horizontally) for creating digital transformation strategy and roll-out . . . get the culture involved from the beginning to promote buy-in and trust

People do not have the right tools or skills to improve the existing process or to use the data to provide insight for continuous improvement of the processes	Employees are trained with tools that will allow them to be empowered and gain insight into data that allows for ongoing continuous improvement	Lack of tools/systems, lack of vision and empowerment, lack of analytical training	People Process Technology	Provide training of critical and useful tools often and to all levels of the organization; specifically those who will use the tools for their daily job. Have training often for everyone. It is not just for the chosen few.
Workers do not have access to data and need IT help to access it. IT is overwhelmed with other priorities, the request is delayed by months, and then the data are no longer needed or valid for the situation.	Overlaying platform that links databases together for easy access of information. Platform is equipped with basic analytical tools that are easy to learn, use, and interpret results, thereby empowering employees.	Systems, accessibility, staffing, conflict of priorities	People Process Technology	Involve people and current processes into the decision making for technology. This will promote buy-in and use of tools. Tools should be easy to use and provide useful insight for employees at all levels.
Employees are not empowered to make improvements (regardless of how simple it is) unless it goes through a long chain of command; therefore, no improvements are made because the process to make improvements is too long	Create an efficient process that empowers employees to make continuous improvement for the good of the organization	Historical and outdated processes, old systems, lack of employee empowerment	People Process Technology	Collaboration on developing/optimizing processes to provide insight and be super user-friendly

(continued)

	Current State	Ideal State	What Is Preventing Ideal State?	Gap People, Pro, Tech, Infr, Other	Bridges
Process	Processes across organization for different departments are performed differently; there is no consistency or accountability even for basic processes that are the same in different departments or within the same department	Incorporate best practices of processes across an organization to instill standardization and consistency	Systems, outdated process, lack of accountability, lack of communication, lack of overall strategic vision	People Process	Collaboration on developing/ optimizing processes to provide insight and be super user-friendly. Incorporate lessons learned and best practices for the organization. Cross train culture to increase diversity and skill sets.
	Processes are limited by the technology that surrounds them	Process designed to be efficient and effective with technology and innovation that supports the process, product or service, and people performing the process. Technology should be considered an enabler for perfection.	Existing systems and technology, lack of innovation with existing system, and processes and technology	Process Technology	Collaboration between users, process owners, and technology people to best understand what type of technology will best fit with the most robust processes and still be in-line with strategic direction of digital transformation
	The same process but in different business units, or within the same business unit, are conducted differently and use different system and databases	Incorporate best practices of processes across an organization to instill standardization and consistency. Integrate the multiple databases under one platform so there is a single source of truth.	Strategic focus and direction across the organization, lack or inefficient training, lack of communication of process changes	Process Technology (depending on process)	Collaboration on developing/ optimizing processes to provide insight and be super user-friendly. Incorporate lessons learned and best practices for the organization. Cross train culture to increase diversity and skill sets.

	Training for several processes differed from trainer to trainer causing inconsistency; specific operational tasks are not explained as being critical to the overall operation	Incorporate best practices of training on all processes resulting in higher standard of work and consistency across employees performing the same task	Lack of SOPs, lack of operational blue prints, and training that is ineffective and lacks standard process and confirmation of correct learning	Process Technology (depending on process)	Develop training standards that are maintained and updated as processes are optimized and technology is implemented. Training standards are a collaboration across the organization and incorporate training practices' best practices.
	Data are not easily accessible, it is difficult to perform analytics or interpret meaning information, and data can also be easily manipulated	A solution that overlays all databases and provides analytical tools that are easy to use and interpret. Prevent data from being manipulated for optical appearances only.	Database silos, de-centralized data system across functional areas and business units. Data difficult to access and analyze so it is "cut and pasted" into Excel and manipulated.	Process Technology	Implement a technology that overlays the existing process, but allows for the process to be optimized and provide robust efficiencies. Cross training and collaboration across organization. Technology should provide easy to access information that is a single point of truth and current real-time data.
Technology	Technology is old and very slow	Latest technology and innovation that is easy to use, powerful, and provides insight to the organization thereby empowering the culture and leaders to have a competitive edge in the market	Strategic vision and direction regarding digitizing the organization and maintaining up-to-date technology and processes	Technology	Update technology for the organization to have a single point of truth, with real-time data that is easily accessible and can easily provide insight to process and business performance. System should overlay the operational excellence umbrella.

(continued)

Current State	Ideal State	What Is Preventing Ideal State?	Gap People, Pro, Tech, Infr, Other	Bridges
Systems can easily be manipulated, impacting the validity of the data	A solution that overlays all databases and provides analytical tools that are easy to use and interpret. Prevent data from being manipulated. Maintain a single source of truth that the entire organization is required to use.	Strategic vision and direction regarding digitizing the organization and maintaining up-to-date technology and processes, lack of processes for accessing data	Process Technology	Update technology for the organization to have a single point of truth, real-time data that is easily accessible and can easily provide insight to process and business performance. System should overlay the operational excellence umbrella.
Database silos across business units and departments within the same function exist	A solution that overlays all databases providing a single point of truth	Strategic vision and direction regarding digitizing the organization	Technology	Update technology for the organization to have a single point of truth, real-time data that is easily accessible and can easily provide insight to process and business performance. System should overlay the operational excellence umbrella.
Workers need IT support to access data which can take forever due to everyone needing their help	A single platform that overlays all databases and is easy to access and use. Analytics that are easy to incorporate to derive insight about the business and/or process.	Lack of IT available resources and manpower, opposing priorities, lack of a system or platform that can be accessed by an empowered employee and not just IT	Technology	IT resources should focus on strategic projects for the organization and employees should have easy access to data/information that will empower them to obtain insight about the process performance. System should overlay the operational excellence umbrella.

Systems are difficult to learn, and with many systems, it is difficult to know what system has what information	A single platform that overlays all databases and is easy to access and use. Analytics that are easy to incorporate to derive insight about the business and/or process.	Strategic vision and direction regarding digitizing the organization	Technology	Implement a user-friendly system with ease to access for everyone. Train employees on how to use and how to gain the most information from the system.
Legacy system has all of the historical and current data—do not want to lose years of information	A single platform that overlays all databases and is easy to access and use. Analytics that are easy to incorporate to derive insight about the business and/or process.	Strategic vision and direction regarding digitizing the organization that will address existing challenges such as legacy systems	People Technology	Implement a system that creates a platform overlaying legacy systems. Understand the needs of the system (ideal state) and think bigger of what is possible . . . then create and implement this platform.
Once data are accessed, there is no tool application to perform analytics, so the data are then "cut and pasted" into Excel to analyze and review	A single platform that overlays all databases and is easy to access and use. Analytics that are easy to incorporate to derive insight about the business and/or process.	Existing technology is not robust enough for the user. No policy for data manipulation.	People Technology	Implement a solution that is equipped with analytical tools that are user-friendly and allow the user to extract insight out of the data easily and efficiently, reporting a single point of truth

(continued)

	Current State	Ideal State	What Is Preventing Ideal State?	Gap People, Pro, Tech, Infr, Other	Bridges
	Daily manufacturing reviews use data collected 24–48 hours prior and all graphical analysis are printed for discussion	Reviews use latest up-to-date information in real-time that is easily retrieved from platform solution	Existing technology is not robust enough for the user and intent of use	Technology	Implement interactive dashboards that are created with real-time data from sensors and other manufacturing equipment and processes
Infrastructure	De-centralized databases and operational excellence strategies across and within business units	A single platform that overlays all databases and is directly tied back to OpEx and strategic objectives	Existing technology and lack of strategic vision and direction regarding digitization	Technology	Implement a solution that creates a platform over all database silos and legacy that create a single point of truth with real-time data across the organization and operational excellence umbrella
	Same function in different departments perform day-to-day tasks differently resulting in different information for strategic review	Incorporate best practices of training on all processes resulting in higher standard of work and consistency across employees performing the same task	Training policies and database silos	People Technology	Create corporate standards using a team of cross collaboration of business units. Insure strategic objectives are clearly communicated across the entire organization at all levels.

Organizational structure does not warrant or encourage collaboration across the organization (vertically and horizontally)	Cross collaboration is a critical component to thrive in the fast-paced changing time. Collaboration is encouraged and required. Process and continuous improvement efforts are designed with collaboration as the foundation.	Historical operational structure, de-centralized, collaboration not encouraged or practiced	People	Re-create the organization structure so collaboration not only exists, but is required
Each functional department has different strategic goals and objectives, often not linking to the overall operational excellence strategic objectives	All business units have strategic goals and objectives that are directly linked back to the organization's overall strategic objectives	Clear strategic vision that is shared across the organization with ongoing communication	People Process	Strong communication of strategic objectives across the entire organization and link all performance evaluations, etc., back to the strategic objectives. All employees should be able to recite the strategic objectives (which are not the same as the mission statement).

Completed Healthcare Example

	Current State	Ideal State	What Is Preventing Ideal State	Gap People, Pro, Tech, Infr, Other	Bridges
People	Multiple platforms or systems that do not link back to process flow of a professional's day to day task (e.g., process flow of nurse)	A single platform that is designed and links with standard process flow and links all systems and platforms under one umbrella for cohesive and fluid access and efficiency for all users of the systems	Multiple databases and platforms not linked to standard process flow	People Process Technology	A platform that overlays the multiple platforms making it seamless for the systems to "talk" with one another so they are easily accessible for all functions of the hospital staff. Overall system or umbrella should provide cohesiveness and efficiency for all users of the system.
	Bilingual (or those for whom English is their second language) staff and employees often experience language barriers and challenges with technology and daily tasks	Technology designed to reduce or eliminate barriers and challenges for those for whom English is not their first language	Existing technology, forms, and input requirements that do not provide the ease of inputting for vernacular reasons	People Process Technology	Develop a template for the systems that take into account vernacular challenges, drop down or pre-populated options, and training of staff to insure effectiveness and efficiency of system and improvements
	Healthcare professionals (docs, nurses) often struggle to work in teams. This is not across the board, but in many areas of healthcare and the hospital.	Employees, professionals, etc., work in a collaborative effort across the organization	Inherent within the individual and the nature of their jobs	People	Training and communication on the importance of a team on the process flow, and transformation plan and journey. It is essential that the organization creates and maintains a collaboration of employees to design and orchestrate the implementation and ongoing continuous improvement success.

	Patient Safety—additional process steps required to maintain governance and patient records can be meticulous and time consuming	Reduce the cycle time of multiple entries of the same information in different locations. Reduce the cycle time of any entry for "common or standard responses"	Multiple systems and the inherent design of the existing systems (out of date for today's requirements and standards)	People Process Technology Infrastructure	Pre-populated SMART phases to eliminate thought process of what is going on with the patient. A platform that overlays all systems so one entry can then populate the other "systems" without additional work or input from the staff.
Process	Instructions are often tailored specifically to the patient. To maintain a record, the professional needs to add the instructions into the system. Some instructions, however, need to be executed, need to be entered into multiple systems. This is time consuming and introduce errors.	One platform or system that allows all of the information or instructions needed to be entered at one time	Multiple databases and platforms	Process Technology	A platform that overlays the multiple platforms making it seamless for the systems to "talk" with one another so they are easily accessible for all functions of the hospital staff
	Multiple platforms and systems cause redundancy in most daily routine processes, resulting in unnecessary "speed bumps" or inhibit the process in other negative ways	Single platform that overlays all of the systems so it eliminates redundancy and allows the process to be more efficient and ultimately more effective	Multiple databases and platforms not linked	Process Technology	A single platform or umbrella that overlays the multiple systems to eliminate redundancy of hospital staff efforts and makes the process flow more efficient and effective

(continued)

Current State	Ideal State	What Is Preventing Ideal State	Gap People, Pro, Tech, Infr, Other	Bridges
Cost variations	Accurate costs and financial model	Single point of truth with real-time data	Process Technology	A single platform or umbrella that overlays the multiple systems to eliminate redundancy of data reporting
Technology Multiple platforms that do not talk with one another	All systems and databases talk with one another and are easily accessible	Platforms used by different departments have varying functions and purposes	Process Technology	A platform that overlays the multiple platforms, making it seamless for the systems to "talk" with one another so they are easily accessible for all functions of the hospital staff
NOTE: see items above for areas where Technology is identified as a "gap"				

Note: Blank forms are available for download at costichgroup.com.

Glossary

artificial intelligence (AI)—the theory and development of computer systems able to perform tasks that normally require human intelligence, such as visual perception, speech recognition, decision making, and translation between languages.

balanced scorecard—a strategy performance management tool; a semi-standard structured report that can be used by managers to keep track of the execution of activities by the staff within their control and to monitor the consequences arising from those actions. Typically used as an indicator of corporate performance against established strategic goals.

big data—extremely large data sets that may be analyzed computationally to reveal patterns, trends, and associations, especially relating to human behavior and interactions.

blockchain—a growing list of records, called blocks, that are linked using cryptography. Each block contains a cryptographic hash of the previous block, a time stamp, and transaction data.

change management—a collective term for all approaches to prepare, support, and help individuals, teams, and organizations in making organizational change. The most common change drivers include technological evolution, process reviews, crisis, and consumer habit changes, as well as pressure from new business entrants, acquisitions, mergers, and organizational restructuring.

computer vision—an interdisciplinary scientific field that deals with how computers can gain high-level understanding from digital images or videos. From the perspective of engineering, it seeks to understand and automate tasks that the human visual system can do.

customer centric—creating a positive consumer experience at the point of sale and post-sale. A customer-centric approach can add value to a company by enabling it to differentiate itself from competitors who do not offer the same experience.

customer centric vs. customer focused—customer-centric organizations offer a number of various products over the life of the customer. Customer-focused organizations offer a single or a limited number of products over the life of the customer. Customer centric is long-term focused. Customer focused is short-term focused.

dashboard—a type of graphical user interface that often provides at-a-glance views of key performance indicators relevant to a particular objective or business process. In other usage, *dashboard* is another name for progress report or report.

data analytics—a process of inspecting, cleansing, transforming, and modeling data with the goal of discovering useful information, informing conclusions, and supporting decision making. Data analysis has multiple facets and approaches, encompassing diverse techniques under a variety of names, and is used in different business, science, and social science domains. In today's business world, data analysis plays a role in making decisions more scientific and helping businesses operate more effectively.

design failure modes and effects analysis (DFMEA)—an analytical technique used by a design-responsible engineer/team as an effective means to identify potential failure modes and their associated causes/mechanisms, assign a risk priority number (RPN), and address ways to mitigate the potential failures through enhanced process controls or increased detection controls.

digital business ecosystem—a distributed, adaptive, open socio-technical system with properties of self-organization, scalability, and sustainability inspired from natural ecosystems. Digital ecosystem models are informed by knowledge of natural ecosystems, especially for aspects related to competition and collaboration among diverse entities. The term is used in the computer industry, the entertainment industry, and the World Economic Forum.

digital customer focus or experience—focuses on the customer, including both front-end services and back-office process optimization that ultimately benefits customers.

Digital Millennium Copyright Act (DMCA)—1998 United States copyright law that implements two 1996 treaties of the World Intellectual Property Organization. It criminalizes production and dissemination of technology, devices, or services intended to circumvent measures that control access to copyrighted works. It also criminalizes the act of circumventing an access control, whether or not there is actual infringement of copyright itself.

digital transformation—the use of new, fast, and frequently changing digital technology to solve problems, whether it be technology or consumer problems.

enterprise resource planning (ERP)—is the integrated management of main business processes, often in real time and mediated by software and technology. ERP is usually referred to as a category of business management software—typically a suite of integrated applications—that an organization can use to collect, store, manage, and interpret data from many business activities.

failure modes and effects analysis (FMEA)—an inductive reasoning (forward logic), single point of failure analysis and is a core task in reliability engineering, safety engineering, and quality engineering. A successful FMEA activity helps identify potential failure modes based on either experience with similar products and processes or common physics of failure logic.

interactive dashboard—a dashboard is a type of graphical user interface that often provides at-a-glance views of key performance indicators relevant to a particular objective or business process. An interactive dashboard allows the users to interact with data, enabling them to navigate and drill down for further analysis and insight.

International Standards Organization (ISO)—an international standard-setting body composed of representatives from various national standards organizations.

key process (or performance) indicators (KPIs)—indicators that directly measure the performance of key processes that affect customer expectations.

lean management—a technique and methodology designed to minimize or eliminate process waste while maximizing the value of the product or service to the customer, without compromising the quality. The term was coined by the Toyota Production System (TPS).

Lean-Six Sigma—a combination of lean management and Six Sigma tools and methodologies designed to improve performance by systematically removing waste and reducing variation.

machine learning (ml)—the study of computer algorithms that improve automatically through experience. It is seen as a subset of artificial intelligence.

marketing analytics—consists of the processes and technologies that enable marketers to evaluate the success of their initiatives, campaigns, and performance in general. Some of the key metrics for marketing analytics include ROI, marketing attribution, and overall marketing effectiveness.

omnichannel (or omni-channel)—defined as a cross-channel sales approach that companies use to connect multiple sales channels and fuse them into one. The goal is to provide their customers a seamless and consistent shopping experience, regardless of whether the customer shops in a brick-and-mortar store, by telephone, or on a website or mobile app.

open-source software (OSS)—a type of computer software in which source code is released under a license in which the copyright holder grants users the rights to use, study, change, and distribute the software to anyone and for any purpose. Open-source software may be developed in a collaborative public manner. Open-source software is a prominent example of open collaboration.

operational excellence (OpEx)—execution of the business strategy that is consistent and efficient across the organization. Operational excellence is evidenced by results. An organization that embeds operational excellence principles into its strategies will have lower operational risk, lower operating costs, and increased revenues, creating value for customers and shareholders.

predictive analytics—a variety of statistical techniques, including data mining, predictive modeling, and machine learning, that analyze current and historical information to make predictions about future or otherwise unknown events.

SAP (Systems, Applications & Products in Data Processing)—a German multinational software corporation that makes enterprise software to manage business operations and customer relations. The company is especially known for its enterprise resource planning software.

Shingo—Shigeo Shingo was a Japanese industrial engineer who was considered the world's leading expert on manufacturing practices and the Toyota Production System. The Shingo transformation process illustrates the critical need to align every business, management, and work system of the organization with the principles of operational excellence.

Six Sigma—a methodology and set of tools designed to reduce variation in a process, thereby increasing efficiencies and overall quality of the product and/or service. The methodology consists of five phases referred to as DMAIC (define, measure, analyze, improve, control).

transformation—a thorough or dramatic change in form or appearance; for an organization, it is a paradigm shift in its "DNA."

Triple Aim (relative to healthcare)—a framework developed by the Institute for Healthcare Improvement (IHI) in 2007 with the intention of assisting healthcare systems in optimizing performance, reducing costs, and improving patient care through a variety of interventions and metrics.

About the Author

Therese Costich, president and managing partner of The Costich Group, has spent more than 25 years in the Digital Transformation, Lean-Six Sigma, and Continuous Improvement world, working with employees from the C-suite to front-line associates, for several Fortune 500 companies. With the focus of the global world becoming smaller and data becoming bigger in every industry, Therese's expertise with operational excellence, business analytics, and digital transformation has guided organizations to become leaders in their industry while sustaining continuous improvement. She has helped organizations thrive in global competitive markets using a digital operational excellence framework that has increased their customer and employee satisfaction, product and service quality, and financial efficiencies, while reducing costs via strategic and tactical process improvements. Therese was the project manager and coauthor for the first edition of *The Black Belt Memory Jogger: A Pocket Guide for Six Sigma Success* published by Goal/QPC. For more information, please visit her website: costichgroup.com.

WHY ASQ?

ASQ is a global community of people passionate about quality, who use the tools, their ideas and expertise to make our world work better. ASQ: The Global Voice of Quality.

FOR INDIVIDUALS

Advance your career to the next level of excellence.

ASQ offers you access to the tools, techniques and insights that can help transform an ordinary career from an extraordinary one.

FOR ORGANIZATIONS

Your culture of quality begins here.

ASQ organizational membership provides the invaluable resources you need to concentrate on product, service and experiential quality and continuous improvement for powerful top-line and bottom-line results.

www.asq.org/why-asq

ASQ
Excellence Through Quality

ASK A LIBRARIAN

Have questions? Looking for answers?
In need of information? Ask a librarian!

Customized research assistance from ASQ's research librarian is one of the many benefits of membership. ASQ's research librarian is available to answer your research requests using the everexpanding library of current and credible resources, including journals, conference proceedings, case studies, and Quality Press publications.

You can also contact the librarian to request permission to reuse or reprint ASQ copyrighted material, such as ASQ journal articles and Quality Press book excerpts.

For more information or to submit a question, visit asq.org/quality-resources/ask-a-librarian.

ASQ
Excellence Through Quality